Making Sense of Marshall Ledbetter

UNIVERSITY PRESS OF FLORIDA

Florida A&M University, Tallahassee
Florida Atlantic University, Boca Raton
Florida Gulf Coast University, Ft. Myers
Florida International University, Miami
Florida State University, Tallahassee
New College of Florida, Sarasota
University of Central Florida, Orlando
University of Florida, Gainesville
University of North Florida, Jacksonville
University of South Florida, Tampa
University of West Florida, Pensacola

MAKING SENSE OF MARSHALL LEDBETTER

The Dark Side of Political Protest

Daniel M. Harrison

University Press of Florida
Gainesville
Tallahassee
Tampa
Boca Raton
Pensacola
Orlando
Miami
Jacksonville
Ft. Myers
Sarasota

VIVA FLORIDA 500
1513-2013

A Florida Quincentennial Book

Library of Congress Control Number: 2014938776
ISBN 978-0-8130-6016-3

The University Press of Florida is the scholarly publishing agency for the
State University System of Florida, comprising Florida A&M University,
Florida Atlantic University, Florida Gulf Coast University, Florida
International University, Florida State University, New College of Florida,
University of Central Florida, University of Florida, University of North
Florida, University of South Florida, and University of West Florida.

University Press of Florida
15 Northwest 15th Street
Gainesville, FL 32611-2079
http://www.upf.com

To my mentors—with thanks

I like songs about drifters, books about the same.
They both make me feel a little less insane.

Modest Mouse, "The World at Large"

Contents

Preface

How tame and unfantastic mere fiction is, compared with history! Actual facts of people are inexpressibly strange.

Aldous Huxley, letter to Harold Raymond, February 21, 1941

This book tells the story of Marshall Robin Ledbetter Jr., an eccentric young man who pulled off one of the oddest stunts in Florida history. In the early morning of June 14, 1991, Marshall, a twenty-two-year-old honors student at Florida State University, staged a one-man assault on the Florida government. He broke into the State Capitol Building in Tallahassee and for the next eight hours occupied the Sergeant at Arms suite. Ledbetter issued a very curious and specific set of demands, claiming his purpose was to draw attention to poverty and homelessness in society.

In the following pages, I provide a sociological interpretation of Ledbetter's break-in, examining its causes, its consequences, and its significance for us today. Most of the information in this book comes from interviews with Ledbetter's friends, family, and acquaintances, newspaper and television coverage of the event, legal documents found in the public record, and Ledbetter's own writings. In telling Ledbetter's story, I have sought, first of all, to get the facts straight. I recognize that some readers with a personal connection to Marshall Ledbetter might find some of aspects of the book troubling. Even so, I hope they will find I have told this story as accurately as possible. I spent seven years researching and three years writing this book, and I understand the gravity of its subject matter. In offering my assessment of this singular incident, I have sought to capture the essence of Marshall Ledbetter as a human being and to tell his story in a way he might appreciate.

This book should appeal to three overlapping sets of readers. As the Ledbetter story is very much a Tallahassee tale, I hope to connect with an audience that has a relationship to Leon County and wants to learn more about its history and culture. Although knowledge of the capitol break-in is unevenly distributed around the state of Florida (and across the Southeast), the event has unquestionably become a part of Tallahassee culture. Indeed, Ledbetter has achieved an almost mythic status in some circles. Those who are unfamiliar with the Ledbetter story can get the complete version here. For readers who already know something about the case, this work should fill in some gaps in the story, provide new material to consider, and offer some ways to better understand what occurred.

In addition to a Florida audience, I also hope to attract a more general set of readers who might simply enjoy a story about youthful rebellion that addresses key political and social issues of our time. Most of the events described in his book took place in the early 1990s, a period that bears interesting resemblances to our own. Falling state revenues, an overextended war machine, the difficulties of young people finding their place in the world, drug and alcohol abuse, and the plight of the mentally ill are all still pressing social concerns. It is my hope that we can gain a better understanding of our own culture by examining the norms and practices of a slightly different place and time.

Finally, this work offers academics a case study in deviance and social control. While Ledbetter's story is certainly an interesting biographical tale in its own right, it also provides a window into the complicated ways that society manages deviant people in real-world situations. The Ledbetter case provides what social researchers call a "natural experiment" for understanding mechanisms of social control in society. It is hoped that readers and researchers in fields such as cultural studies, criminology, history, psychology, and my own discipline of sociology might be as fascinated by the Ledbetter story as I have been. By seeking to understand this extraordinary incident and its cascading effects, by examining the various dimensions to the Ledbetter case over time, and by studying the competing discourses surrounding it and the social fields that created them, this book presents a vivid sociological account of a deviant career.

Making Sense of Marshall Ledbetter

Intruder at the Capitol

I just had to know, inside, if I could do it. Haven't you ever wondered that, about something?

Marshall Ledbetter, "11-17-01"

You were high on freedom, literally carried away with it.
. . . If it was midnight and you were seized with the desire
to pile into a car and drive from Selma to Montgomery and
climb on the roof of the governor's mansion . . . then you
did it.

John Lewis, *Walking with the Wind*

Ruby Dean Dennis, a custodian at the State Capitol Building in Tallahassee, Florida, arrived at work on Friday, June 14, 1991, shortly after 7:00 a.m. Just like any other workday, Dennis organized her janitorial cart, got her supplies together, and started her morning routine.

At about 7:15, the forty-one-year-old woman made her way up to the fourth floor of the capitol building. As she was pushing the cart down the corridor, Dennis looked down and noticed something out of place.[1] She saw a pair of denim shorts, covered in paint, balled up on the floor. This seemed very odd. Dennis stopped for a moment to consider how the shorts might have gotten there. With some trepidation, she continued down the hallway. Then she saw a pair of flip-flops.

Dennis looked to her left as she rounded the end of the corridor and noticed that a few more things were out of place. Over toward the Senate chambers, the ornamental legal tomes and other books about Florida that were normally on display were strewn all about the lobby. A number of information signs had also been knocked over.

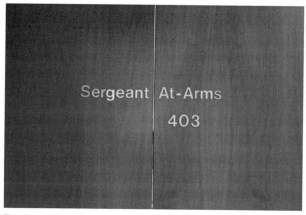

The door to the Sergeant at Arms office, which Marshall Ledbetter occupied during the morning of June 14, 1991. Photo courtesy of Jason Flom.

It was at this moment that Ruby Dennis knew this was not going to be any ordinary day. She was standing in front of Room 403, the Sergeant at Arms suite. The office was always one of her first stops of the day. Dennis tried her key in the door. She could unlock it, but it wouldn't open. Something was blocking it from the inside. Dennis peered through the half-inch gap in the doorway. She couldn't see anything. She tried again to open the heavy wooden door. It wouldn't budge. Although she had no idea who or what might be inside, she was determined to find out. She pushed against the door a little harder. It opened a few inches.

Then, just as Dennis was straining to peek her head through the doorway, a sizable, heavy object came zipping in out of nowhere, smashing to bits on the other side of the door. Liquid and glass went flying. "Something went over my face and I started to run," Dennis would later tell the police.[2] Now quite panicked, she beat a hasty retreat to the third floor, where she found a co-worker and told her what had happened. Together they went to notify the Capitol Police at their office on the second floor of the building.

Sergeant William Hartsfield and bomb technician Jesse Lovett were talking in the Capitol Police office when Ruby and her co-worker appeared and informed them about what was going on upstairs. Lovett had been called in earlier that morning to investigate a strange-looking object found near the south entrance to the building.[3] He and Harts-field were trying to figure out how it got there and what it meant. The officers listened to Dennis's story and then rushed to the Sergeant at Arms suite. They couldn't gain entry either.

Ruby provided a statement of what had occurred and was sent to get medical attention. She was then excused for the rest of the day. When she got to her Tallahassee home, just off Capitol Circle Northeast, she found the property crawling with newspaper reporters. Somehow the media had found out where she lived. They were tramping around her yard, peering in her windows, hounding her for a comment.

"Go away. I can't talk," she told them.[4]

A Florida State Awakening

The faculty in our State University System are some of the
most intelligent people that I have ever met on this earth.

Marshall Ledbetter, live on *WFSU* radio, June 10, 1991

Rebels perceived that the campus was not all. Outside its
gates stood a vital world of economics, politics, and the
arts, more real than the fun and games of football. . . . But
in fighting for power, they did not forget the purposes of
the university. They tried to make real contact with the
minds of the professors, in class and out. Although sometimes negligent about their assignments and cavalier about
exams, rebels took ideas and their consequences seriously.

Helen Horowitz, *Campus Life*

The intruder was twenty-two-year-old Marshall Robin Ledbetter Jr.,
who was just coming down from one hell of a bender. The erstwhile
honors student had been attending Florida State off and on since 1987.

Ledbetter was born in 1969 under the glare of the Florida sun in Win-
ter Haven, about an hour's drive south of Orlando. He grew up in the
adjacent town of Auburndale. His parents were Marshall and Sharon
Ledbetter. In many respects his was a typical middle-class upbringing.
Marshall Jr. was one of four children. He has an older sister, Christina,
and a pair of twins, Arlen and Carla, four and a half years younger.[1]
Marshall's father worked as a science and mathematics professor at
Polk Community College (now Polk State College) in Winter Haven.
In 1980 Sharon and Marshall Sr. opened Marshall's Camera—a small
photography and camera shop in downtown Auburndale. It was very
much a joint business venture between husband and wife. Through the

Marshall Ledbetter, age 1.
Photo courtesy of Sharon
Graham.

couple's blood, sweat, and tears, over time what had started as a hobby in the Ledbetters' home became through hard work and long hours a thriving small business. This was no easy accomplishment in America at the end of the twentieth century, especially with four children.

Sharon Ledbetter would open the shop in the morning while Marshall Sr. was teaching and then stay at the business until he took over later in the day. Often they would work at the store together, with Sharon at the front counter and Marshall Sr. in the back, developing film, for example, or fixing cameras. The Ledbetter children would go to Marshall's Camera after school and do their homework in the room in the back at a table before being allowed to watch their favorite shows on television. Fritz Krawchuk,[2] who roomed with Marshall at FSU, remembers Ledbetter's parents as "very nice and super friendly."[3]

Ledbetter had long been noted for his above-average intelligence. His first grade teacher, Nell Little, says young Marshall was "one of the smartest kids I ever taught."[4] In his junior year, Marshall scored high enough on the PSAT to qualify as a National Merit Scholar. As a senior he earned a combined math and verbal score of 1480 on the

Marshall Ledbetter, age 16. Photo courtesy of Sharon Graham.

SAT, placing him in the 99th percentile. He was a smart young man with an "IQ around 170."[5] Auburndale High School yearbook pictures show Marshall smiling and laughing. He was a member of the Science Club and the National Honor Society. Ledbetter's high school principal, Rusty Payne, remembers Marshall as an "outspoken" student who "never did anything strange."[6] In his senior year, 1986–87, in an attempt to get a jump on college, Marshall took a full load of classes at Polk Community College.[7]

Marshall arrived in Tallahassee at the beginning of the 1987 fall semester as an eighteen-year-old honors student. His mother says that Marshall had always wanted to attend Florida State.[8] She says that, as a prospective student, he had toured other schools, including the

University of South Florida and the University of Florida, but it was Florida State University that reeled him in. His National Merit Scholarship paid the costs of tuition, while his parents covered Marshall's room and board. He was five feet, eleven inches tall and weighed about 150 pounds, with hazel eyes and brown hair. Given the academic credits he had accumulated at the Polk Community College, he was classified as a sophomore.

On campus, Ledbetter was welcomed at Landis Hall, the honors dormitory. Landis Hall is located in the center of campus, one hundred yards south of Strozier Library, across from Landis Green. In 1987, the first and third floors of Landis Hall were for males and the second and fourth floors were for females. On the fifth floor, where Marshall lived, half the residents were male and half female. A shared common room with a television was located in the middle of the space, separating male from female wings.

Tallahassee is a fine location for a university. Of Creek derivation, the word *Tallahassee* translates into English as "old town" or "abandoned fields." Human beings have been living in the area for about

Landis Hall, the honors dormitory of Florida State University, where Marshall Ledbetter lived during the 1987–88 school year. Photo courtesy of Jason Flom.

ten thousand years.[9] The only Confederate state capital east of the Mississippi not captured by the Union army during the Civil War, this medium-sized city is today one of the more livable metropolitan areas in the South. Tallahassee offers a unique blend of community and urbanism. Its main function is as the state capital. As the state of Florida has changed, so has Tallahassee. Yet even with all the growth, traffic, and often noxious machinery of state politics, one still finds in Tallahassee pockets of small-town charm. The region's traditions and the city's proximity to the coast create a vibrant social milieu. With all the students, educators, and state workers, progressive sexual politics, and a thriving music and arts scene, Tallahassee and surrounding Leon County are considered among the more liberal places in the state.

After living in Tallahassee, some people find they can't move away. As former *Tallahassee Democrat* writer Steve MacQueen comments, "It's one of those college towns that has a way of pulling you back."[10] National Public Radio commentator and Florida State University English professor Diane Roberts, herself a Tallahassee native, observes that hometown has a "dreamlike quality" about it.[11] She says Tallahassee "has the ironic and slightly haunted atmosphere of a place where every patch of ground holds a story."[12]

Interesting folktales and micro-narratives punctuate Tallahassee lore. Stories about Florida's first American governor (war hero and populist Andrew "Old Hickory" Jackson),[13] the Tallahassee Bus Boycott, Jim Morrison (one of FSU's most famous students, if not graduates),[14] the "Night of the Bayonets" at FSU campus during the Vietnam War, serial killer Ted Bundy's brutal slaying of two sorority sisters, media mogul Ted Turner's vast acreage on the outskirts of town, funk master George Clinton's longtime residency, and "King Love," aka Kamal Yousseff, the former doctor who lost his mind and became a sidewalk preacher—these are just some of the fascinating stories and characters you learn about if you stick around Tallahassee long enough.

But there is also a dark side to life in Leon County. Residents are segregated by enduring systems of race and class stratification, which can be very cruel if one is on the wrong end of the hierarchy.[15] Homeless people gather on the edge of FSU campus, begging for spare change on Tennessee Street, whiling away the daylight hours before the shelter opens. Florida State's more affluent students cruise around in new BMWs, putting the ten-year-old Hondas driven by faculty to shame.[16] When the legislature is in session every spring from March to May, Tallahassee experiences a perceptible increase in glitz, glamour, and conspicuous consumption, and one can discern (if only briefly) just who really holds the reins of power in the state.

Marshall Ledbetter came to Florida's capital city from the relatively small town of Auburndale in central Florida. He was raised in a fairly conservative household. His mother says that all four Ledbetter children were taught to be contributing, responsible members of the family. "We raised four very talented, wonderful children," she says.[17] Yet she also wonders whether Marshall Jr. had not been socially mature enough when he headed off to Florida State University. In retrospect, she says, he might have been better off at a school closer to home.

Jasper Boehmke,[18] who lived with Marshall during their freshman year at Landis Hall, says Ledbetter had been "very straight laced" and was "a relatively normal person" in high school. It was rumored he had never tried alcohol, let alone drugs, before arriving in Tallahassee.[19] Boehmke and others at Landis found Marshall to be a likable, funny science geek, the sort of kid who liked to read novelists like Kurt Vonnegut and Phillip K. Dick and also physicist Richard Feynman in his spare time.[20] Boehmke says Ledbetter was "whip-cracking smart."[21] Lanora Mahler,[22] who with her boyfriend shared an apartment off campus with Marshall during his second year at Florida State, remembers Marshall as "a very funny guy, and really, *really* smart. . . . Ninety-nine percent of the people couldn't keep up."[23]

Another friend, Andrew Arvesen, recalls having a number of "memorable and strange experiences with Marshall" at Florida State. As an example he mentioned Marshall's incremental theft of an entire four-person setting of institutional crockery from the campus cafeteria. Ledbetter would present the cups and dishes as a gift to his older sister, Christina, on her wedding day.[24] In another prank, Marshall devised a surefire method of getting soda out of the Landis Hall Coke machine.

"You had to tip the Coke machine over to a certain angle," recalls Jonathan Lammers, another Landis Hall resident and one of Marshall's closest friends during this period.[25] It was a difficult balancing act. On one occasion, Marshall didn't get the physics quite right and the thing fell over, immobilizing him completely. On the way to the ground, the machine hit Marshall in the face, creating a lasting scar on the left side of his mouth.

Ledbetter enjoyed the campus and Tallahassee's surrounding environment. He was an avid mountain biker and naturalist and often went on impromptu field trips in the woods. Occasionally he and three or four others from Landis Hall would pile into Eric Witherspoon's Chevy S-10 Blazer for late-night off-roading sessions.[26] They would cruise around Apalachicola National Forest about ten miles southwest of town, driving too fast on the dirt tracks, stopping occasionally to gaze at the stars and marvel at the relative wilderness.

Other activities involved consuming large quantities of alcoholic beverages. It didn't take long for Ledbetter to get initiated into FSU's drinking culture. Though he was inexperienced relative to his peers, Marshall quickly made up for lost time. He fell in with a crowd of other bright students determined to bolster FSU's reputation as one of the country's top party schools. According to Fritz Krawchuk, Marshall became a "raving binge drinker" during his first year at FSU.[27]

Ledbetter was a "geeky guy with a *Far Side* sense of humor," recalls Andrew Arvesen.[28] Marshall loved to play chess and was very good at it. He could be counted on to contribute wild and zany ideas to any conversation. Friend Bert Peppe[29] says Marshall might be at a party and suddenly ask the group: "What would happen if you dropped ten squirrels out of an airplane quickly followed by ten cats? Would the cats ever be able to catch the squirrels?"[30] It's the sort of Monty Pythonesque inquiry that fellow slackers in Ledbetter's generation would love to debate. Arvesen remembers Marshall saying crazy things but in a "totally sincere" sort of way.

Ledbetter was known particularly for his ability to rant (often under the influence of drugs and alcohol) on and on about, for example, the injustice of a certain situation, the meaning of a particular book, the social and economic implications of an idea, or the ignorance and pomposity of the powerful. At times Ledbetter's rhetoric came close to what Karl Marx called the "ruthless criticism of everything existing." Although his rapid-fire rhetoric did sometimes digress into bizarrely nested tangents, much of what Ledbetter said did often make considerable sense and also generated a lot of laughs. Lanora Mahler remembers that "Marshall was a funny guy." She says his rants were "meant to amuse people. And they did amuse."[31]

In addition to his comic performances, Ledbetter cultivated a rather libertarian, more specifically anarchical, worldview during his early days at FSU. He became anti-authoritarian on a primary, instinctual level. This ideological transformation was fueled not only by books but also by music such as Dead Kennedys, Suicidal Tendencies, Metallica, the Clash, the Sex Pistols, and Motörhead. Marshall also enjoyed funk music like Parliament and was a huge fan of rap music, particularly Public Enemy.

With such music as his sound track, in the spring of his first year Marshall also found a new religion: slackness. He eased up on his schoolwork, kept on with the drinking, and started smoking marijuana. By that fall he was also experimenting with psychedelic mushrooms. Fritz Krawchuk says Marshall "loved mushrooms."[32] In general, it seems that Marshall was always on the lookout for a good time. According to Jasper Boehmke, whenever there was a party, Marshall would be there.[33] Yet casual partying wasn't enough for Marshall. If people were drinking beer, Boehmke says, Marshall would "shotgun" a beer (that is, punch a hole in the bottom, lift the pull tab, and suck the beer out). If people were doing "whippets" (balloons of nitrous oxide), Marshall would inhale two in quick succession, then jump up and down trying to pass out. Marshall had a "level of intensity one step beyond that of most people," Boehmke recalls.[34]

Such behavior would cause some consternation with potential love interests and often handicapped Marshall's attempts at finding a girlfriend. Although he was a smart young man, Marshall was always somewhat awkward with the ladies. Boehmke says that he "never saw Marshall date in my entire life."[35] Lanora Mahler mentions it was a shame Marshall didn't have many girlfriends or "quality hookups" at FSU, since he was "kind of cute."[36] But Ledbetter's handsomeness could not compensate for his often strange behavior. Marshall would begin to "put the moves on you and then start to rant about something, like, 'George III was a good king!'" says Mahler.

During Marshall's second year at Florida State, it appears that the freedom of being away from home, the pleasures of life in Tallahassee, and the partying got the better of him. When Marshall's grades were submitted at the end of the spring 1989 term, they were not at all good. He had flunked out. Marshall gathered his belongings and left Tallahassee. He returned to Auburndale, enrolled at Polk Community College, and began work as a high school substitute teacher.[37]

The Monarchy Days

You and me lying on the tile floor
trying to keep cool, restless all night
sweating out the poison as the temperature climbs.

The Mountain Goats, "Have to Explode"

What I loved in particular about the Monarchy Party
was that it was an assemblage of freaks from all different
spheres.

Marshall Ledbetter, "Tales of Psychoboy," October 1, 1996

In the fall of 1990, Marshall moved back to Tallahassee and resumed his studies at Florida State. He had completed his Associate of Arts degree at Polk Community College in Winter Haven earlier that year. Now classified as a junior, he was majoring in biological science. Marshall had managed to get his act together. He had even regained his National Merit Scholarship. Living off campus back in 1988–89 had not gone particularly well, so he was back in the dorms. He first stayed at Smith Hall, on the west side of campus, and spent four months there before moving to Cawthon Hall.

One of Marshall's favorite classes was with Dr. Walter R. Tschinkel, a Distinguished Research Professor and a leading expert in fire ants, one of Florida's most vicious insects. After the capitol break-in, Professor Tschinkel told the *Florida Flambeau* that Ledbetter "was brighter than most of the other students and had a rather quirky sense of humor. He seemed genuine to me because he thought about a lot of things and took them seriously."[1] In 2011, Dr. Tschinkel still remembered Marshall from the insect biology class in the spring of 1991. He says Marshall was "very smart and did well . . . the kind of student that we look for."[2] Marshall earned an A, the second-highest grade in the class.[3] Tschinkel says that Marshall was "imaginative," very interested in the course material, and would often chat with him after class. Tschinkel remembers this was often "quite smart conversation," but occasionally "quite bizarre," involving references to "spacemen, and so on."[4]

Marshall was gripped by the subject matter. Not the type of student to passively absorb information in the classroom, Ledbetter fully embraced the learning experience. He would embark on nighttime insect-collecting expeditions around Tallahassee with his etherized kill jar, returning hours later to share the specimens with friends. The show-and-tell would be met with mixed reaction. "Those are just bugs, Marshall," his good friend Bert Peppe joked.[5]

In thinking of the student subculture at FSU at that time, one is reminded of Richard Linklater's 1991 film *Slacker,* which documents the postmodern intellectual and social scene among twenty-somethings in circa 1989 Austin, Texas. Disenchanted with their schooling and day jobs, the slacker youth of 1990s America found existential sustenance in idiosyncratic hobbies and amusements which often became obsessions. Linklater's bright, witty, and underemployed cast of characters surely had their counterparts among Ledbetter's cohort in Tallahassee in the late 1980s and early 1990s, and perhaps still today. To steal a line from Woody Allen, Ledbetter and his friends didn't let schooling interfere with their education.

Yet it seems that Professor Tschinkel's class was the only bright spot on an otherwise bleak horizon. Marshall's parents were starting to worry about their son. He had recently informed them of his interest in something called "virtual reality" and his plans to travel around the United States making videotapes spliced together from his rants.[6] While such an effort might sound a little like Ken Kesey and the Merry Pranksters touring the country back in 1964—making movies, recording sounds, and generally freaking people out along the way—Marshall's parents were not enthused. His father also could not fathom Marshall's request to him to "rent an abandoned strip mine to provide space for the videotaping of a rock concert that could be broadcast by satellite throughout the world."[7]

Marshall Ledbetter (*right*) and friend Eric Witherspoon at a house party in Tallahassee during the fall 1990 semester. Photo courtesy of Eric Witherspoon.

Things came to a head at the beginning of April 1991, in the final weeks of the spring term. It was at this moment that Marshall Robin Ledbetter Jr. abandoned his formal education and fell prey to more primal forces. Since his return to Tallahassee, Marshall had been partying quite heavily once again, to the detriment of his schoolwork. He was listening to a considerable amount of militant rap music, not just Public Enemy—then at the vanguard of politically charged or "conscious" rap—but also a more militant rap group made up of real death-row inmates, called The Lifers.[8]

Rap music was an important part of Marshall's life. Given the occasional positive feedback he would get from his friends, Marshall had aspirations of becoming a rapper himself. The stage name he chose for himself was DNA. Although there are no extant Ledbetter raps available from that time period, here is a one he concocted five years later:

> In this brutal world I'm assailed by ideology and theology
> But none of our leaders seem to know sociobiology
> Merely whipping up hysteria against a rival nation-state
> And if that doesn't work, they'll find someone else to hate
> "Communists" "Crack heads" "Liberals" "Fascists" "Welfare mothers"
> Everyone is labeled instead of being sisters and brothers
> I sometimes wonder if it has been this way in every day and age
> Wasn't it Shakespeare who said "All the world's a stage"?
> And does this mean we'll elect those best able to deceive?
> And having lied their way up to the top, are they able to receive
> Any true enlightenment or did they just learn to thieve?[9]

With dreams of being a rapper, Marshall regaled his Tallahassee associates with plans similar to those he had described to his father. John Griffin, another member of Ledbetter's Landis Hall cohort, remembers that one day Marshall borrowed his telephone to make an expensive long-distance phone call to NASA at Cape Canaveral asking how much would it cost to rent the space shuttle. Ledbetter's plan was to launch himself into space and then host a rap concert from the space shuttle.[10] DNA would be the headlining act.

Although it is unclear if it generated any business, Ledbetter formed a Tallahassee-based public-relations firm called Indole-Alkaloid Productions, a reference to the chemical makeup of psilocybin mushrooms.[11] Ledbetter started to think of himself as an up-and-coming music producer. One day Marshall and Lanora Mahler went to Capitol Eurocars, a Mercedes-Benz dealership on the west side of Tallahassee. Ledbetter raised some eyebrows from the lot jockeys and would have been a topic of conversation for days to come after approaching a salesman and trying to negotiate the purchase a new Mercedes-Benz with nothing but royalties from a yet-to be-recorded rap album.[12]

Every aspiring artist needs a muse, and for Marshall it was pop icon and former cheerleader Paula Abdul. Ledbetter's adoration for Abdul was permanently inscribed on the back of his blue denim jacket, which read "DNA ♥ Paula Abdul." Marshall would wear it with pride. At the time, Abdul was just emerging as America's newest "dance-pop princess."[13] Ledbetter first confided his love for Abdul to his close friends. He told them he really wished he could be rapper MC Skat Kat, a feline cartoon character and Abdul's dance partner in her 1990 music video "Opposites Attract."[14]

Marshall's identification with MC Skat Kat—likely developed through sustained periods of intoxication and sleep deprivation coupled with too much MTV—is understandable. Just like MC Skat Kat, Ledbetter liked to move fast and party all night. They both were always broke, and liked to smoke cigars.

Marshall's fascination with Abdul herself is more puzzling. Friends couldn't understand why Ledbetter was so enamored with the pop star. Jonathan Lammers says Abdul "personified the blandness and shallowness of pop culture at the time—the same sorts of things that Marshall was ranting against."[15] According to another Ledbetter friend, Chris Boose, the attraction was more basic. Boose says Ledbetter's fascination with Abdul was "completely sexual." Marshall "wanted to bang Paula Abdul."[16]

In a completely different kind of cultural exploration, Marshall had been researching his genealogy and discovered he was part Native American. Soon he began to refer to himself as Raven and would tell his friends he was the local equivalent of a Native American clown dancer. The Raven is a revered totem in Native American folklore. It represents "magic and sorcery, transformational powers, guidance for deeper understanding of the shadow self, [and] courage and comfort with the darkness."[17] Clown dancers play an important role in Native American culture. Their main purpose is to mock everyone and everything around them. The clown dancer may be considered to be a kind of aboriginal court jester, another figure with whom Ledbetter would identify. The role of clown dancer was fitting for Marshall. Most of the photographs we have of him show him smiling or laughing. It is well documented that he loved a good joke.

Even though Marshall wasn't spending much time in a classroom, he was being creative in other ways. He invented a comic strip called

Marshall Ledbetter created a number of "Mushroom Cop" comics during the spring 1991 semester. He mailed some of them to the *Florida Flambeau* in an attempt to get the paper to publish them. This particular image was printed by the *Flambeau* on the Monday after Ledbetter's takeover of the capitol. It is used with permission of the *FSView*.

"Mushroom Cop," which he photocopied at Kinkos and distributed throughout town. Not everyone was impressed by the quality of the artwork. Tallahassee business owner and Ledbetter acquaintance Gregory Cohen says the "Mushroom Cop" comics were "terrible . . . the worst doodles you could ever imagine."[18] Jonathan Lammers disagrees. He thinks it was the cleverest thing Marshall did during that period. Lammers says that "Mushroom Cop allowed Marshall to focus his acid wit on whatever subject moved him. The drawings were very simple, but very effective. And they were wickedly funny.[19] *Florida Flambeau* editor Ron Matus recalls Ledbetter trying to get the newspaper to publish his drawings: "Marshall came into the *Flambeau* one day to pitch a cartoon called 'Mushroom Cop.' I seem to remember him saying, 'You know it's better than Fat Rabbit, man! You know it is!' (Which it probably was)."[20]

Ledbetter was also immersing himself in the writings of Timothy Leary, the former Harvard psychologist. Leary was one of the more articulate advocates of the mind-expanding properties of psychedelic drugs in the 1960s. An icon of the counterculture, Leary encouraged a whole generation of young people to "Turn on, Tune In, Drop Out." He also had a number of quite serious run-ins with the law and was even invited to John Lennon and Yoko Ono's "Bed In" protest in Montreal in 1969. A generation later, Leary found another receptive audience in youthful rebels like Ledbetter, who had been born just as the cultural struggles of the 1960s were boiling over. But Leary's message had changed over the years. Although Leary did not completely dissociate himself from his earlier advocacy of psychedelic substances, in the 1990s he prophesied comparable mind expansion through computer-generated "virtual reality" instead. Marshall was all ears.

Marshall was also expressing more than a passing interest in the Church of the SubGenius, the satirical, anti-religious pseudo-cult lead by Bob Dobbs. To quote from their sacred text, *The Book of the SubGenius*, the Church of the SubGenius is "an order of Scoffers and Blasphemers, dedicated to Total Slack."[21] The church's main doctrinal teaching is to get something for nothing. Its ideological system is tethered to a bizarre cosmology conceived over the course of too many LSD trips. As a metaphysics, this means it can contain a grain of paranoid truth if one is in the wrong frame of mind. The church advocates putting the screws to the system in as many ways possible and publishes how-to guides for ironic proselytizing and independent local action. If you have access to a photocopier, a stapler, and a pocket full of dimes, you too can become an acolyte for Bob Dobbs, the anti-hero of brilliant underachievers. Marshall was a devoted adherent. He not only appreciated the church's conspiratorial theorizing, but in a kind of slacker jujitsu managed to turn SubGenius teachings against the organization itself. One day he ordered twelve copies of *The Book of the SubGenius* from Reverend Ivan Stang's post office box in Dallas and then mailed in a bad check.[22]

In addition to the Church of the SubGenius, Marshall would have been familiar with the antics of the Principia Discordia group.[23] This outfit was an even earlier outgrowth of 1960s "acid head" ideology that counted famed science fiction writer Robert Anton Wilson among its members. Principia Discordia might be said to have paved the way for what the Church of the SubGenius would later accomplish. Writer Adam Gorightly comments that "Discordianism—i.e. sowing the seeds of chaos as a means of achieving a higher state of awareness—is a perpetual game, better known in some quarters as Operation Mindfuck."[24] In these groups, Ledbetter would have found an ideology and a set of practices at once reflective and constitutive of his own. He was also influenced by social forces closer to home.

The Marshall Ledbetter story cannot be properly understood without discussing the influence of number of inventive friends at FSU who had formed an alternative student government group called the Monarchy Party. The group had been founded by Jonathan Lammers, Andrew Arvesen, Chuck Powell, and Gregory Cohen in the spring of 1989. Arvesen—who reigned as the Monarchy Party's King Andrew—says that he and his friends formed the Monarchy Party because they just "couldn't vote for any of these jerks" then shamelessly manipulating student government.[25] The Monarchists argued that, for years, fraternities and sororities had rigged the student government system to serve their own interests, claiming a mandate from the student body despite low (less than 10 percent) voter turnout. According Lammers, the Greeks were so entrenched in student government that "they might as well have been a monarchy."[26] The Monarchy Party attempted to take back student government. They ridiculed the ruling Seminole Party and Pan-Hellenic Council and "made them sound hollow."[27]

The Monarchists would adorn themselves with all sorts of props and accoutrements as they enacted their symbolic struggles. Dressed in colorful, flamboyant costumes, they aped the style and manner of the Old Regime before the Revolution. They donned leopard-skin jackets, prancing about FSU campus wearing tights and fake crowns. They issued funny directives in fake English accents, like "Eat candy, pigs," while tossing jelly beans to the opposition in a debate.[28]

Although at the height of its influence the Monarchy Party held only fourteen out of sixty student government seats at Florida State, it exerted a considerable cultural influence on campus life. According to former *Tallahassee Democrat* reporter Steve MacQueen, the Monarchy Party offered a "hilarious, brutal lampooning of student government."[29] He says the group was adept at "tweaking the power structure" and that they "viciously mocked and satirized" the whole football- and fraternity-dominated campus scene.[30]

The Monarchists were not only adept performers; they were also excellent writers and propagandists. They produced a number of satirical student newspapers, including *The King's English* and *Rolling Throne* (the latter with the motto "All the News That Fits the Prince").[31] Articles for these publications were hammered out during furious six-hour group writing sessions in the FSU computer lab. They were printed as newsprint pamphlets and freely distributed by the thousands across campus and around Tallahassee.

In the early 1990s, Ledbetter's friend and Landis Hall dorm mate John Wells wrote a paper for a graduate-level English class about the Monarchy Party. Wells stated that the party was a "subversive, radical student movement that is far more threatening to the cushy status quo of the present student government than our elected officials would care to admit."[32] He argued that the Monarchists were "steeped in history" and provided the Florida State campus with intelligent, well-informed satire.

"We did our homework," agrees Arvesen. He also reveals that the Monarchists gained much of their inspiration from a 1970 article written by Hunter S. Thompson for *Rolling Stone* and titled "Freak Power in the Rockies." In that essay, the icon of 1960s satire and excess called upon all the "Freaks" of the world—whom he described as the "Heads, criminals, anarchists, beatniks, poachers, Wobblies, bikers, and Persons of Weird Persuasion"—to "come out of their holes" and get involved in the political process. Thompson named this strategy the Aspen Technique. He defined it as a political approach that involves "neither opting out of the system, nor working within it, but calling its bluff, by using its strength to turn it back on itself."[33]

In producing their funny and caustic spectacles, the Monarchists drew upon a considerable repertoire of cultural ideas and practices, role models and historical figures. Regarding the efficacy of the group, Cohen confesses that the Monarchy Party was not interested in real political power. He says that there was "no point in taking control of student government. Winning was not the point. Proving that we could do so more creatively was the point."[34] Yet Arvesen points out that, interestingly enough, all three of the Monarchists' top demands during the early 1990s—having a snack bar in the student union, moving the fraternities off campus, and closing down Woodward Avenue—were incorporated into FSU's strategic plan and would eventually become reality.

Marshall didn't have an official role in the Monarchy Party, but he was an active member. Arvesen remembers that Ledbetter would attend and speak up at the meetings. Yet he says Ledbetter had an independent streak about him. He describes Marshall as a "fellow traveler, on his own trip . . . always doing his own thing."[35] The Monarchy Party at Florida State University had a tremendous impact on Marshall Ledbetter's identity, worldview, and aspirations. He would look back upon the Monarchy days as among the best of his life.

Vision Quest

Encounters with psychedelic plants throw into question the entire world view of the dominant culture.

Terence McKenna, *Food of the Gods*

Hey, Mr. Responsible Citizen! Guess what? There're shamans creeping around out there. At night. Out there. In the dark. And their eyes are dilated. They can see better than you.

Marshall Ledbetter, "11-17-01"

In February 1991, Ledbetter and some friends made the six-hour drive from Tallahassee to New Orleans to celebrate Mardi Gras. Ledbetter financed the trip with a number of credit cards he had recently received in the mail.[1] At some point during the excursion to the Big Easy, Ledbetter suffered an "extreme case of 'whippet frostbite' on his hands after consuming $150 worth of nitrous oxide chargers."[2] Friend Deon Gondron[3] comments: "I still laugh at the phrase 'whippet frostbite.' It was a perfectly accurate description of what occurred. The air in the little nitrous cylinders was compressed, and when you cracked them open (using a crude plastic device attached to a balloon—these were being sold legally all over New Orleans at the time), the gas that was released was really, really cold. Marshall cracked open so many cylinders in a row that he, quite literally, developed 'whippet frostbite' on his hands."[4]

At the time, "whippets" were a recreational drug legally available not just in New Orleans but all over the country. The ability of laughing gas to do considerably more than just distract one's mind during a root canal had been known at least since the investigations of Harvard psychologist and philosopher William James in the 1870s.[5] More than a century later, law enforcement and others would refer to the recreational use of nitrous oxide as "hippy crack." When whippets were legal, partygoers would buy cartridges by the carton at head shops and kitchen supply stores. A large rubber balloon would be attached to a metal charger (or cracker), and when the seal was broken the balloon would inflate. The user would then inhale all the gas out of the balloon, before seeing stars and going completely numb. The whole experience may be likened to the pharmacological equivalent of being hit with a sledgehammer. Some particularly desperate addicts have been known to huff the nitrous oxide out of whipped-cream canisters during late-night excursions to the grocery store. If you ever have tried to use an aerosol can of whipped cream only to have your strawberry shortcake coated with an oozy sticky discharge instead of creamy foam, it is likely your nitrous was pilfered in such a manner.

By the time of the road trip to New Orleans—roughly halfway through that spring semester—Marshall had probably already sabotaged any hope of a satisfactory ending to the term. But if he had not yet done so, that outcome would be soon apparent. Marshall stopped going to class, did not attend his final examinations, and did not register for any more classes at Florida State University.

Spring in Tallahassee is a marvelous time of year. Students peel off their clothes, play hacky sack, toss Frisbees, and sunbathe on Landis Green. Mountain bikes are tuned up and sea kayaks christened in the rivers around Tallahassee and in the Gulf waters off Alligator Point. Nature beckons and the rainy season begins. Answering the call of the wild, at the beginning of April 1991, Marshall went on a self-described "vision quest." For readers unfamiliar with the term, a vision quest is a spiritual journey to find one's place in the world. According to psychologists Carl Jung and Joseph Campbell, the vision quest lies deep in our evolution as a species.[6] Many different cultures have their own version of the vision quest. It was even central to the Muscogee Creeks, who used to inhabit the land in and around Tallahassee where Ledbetter just happened to be.

The vision quest is a journey taken by young people as they make "their individual journeys into nature."[7] According to the Creeks, "Each individual's visions were his or her property and were highly respected. The vision could result in pointing toward a pathway in life and it could also reveal a specific wisdom, direction, or a gift such as a song."[8] Although Marshall's vision quest wasn't exactly the same sort of cultural experience as this, it would nonetheless become essential to forging the pathway of his life. For Marshall Ledbetter, the vision quest would be a remarkable transformative experience.

Not all vision quests involve the use of mind-altering substances (for example, sweat-lodge ceremonies), but the use of psychedelic compounds is often a crucial part of the journey. In Mexico, the use of psilocybin (also known as "magic" or "psychedelic") mushrooms in vision quests dates back four millennia.[9] In the United States, mushrooms have been known on the drug scene since the early 1960s. The individual most responsible for creating social awareness about the wonders of psychedelic mushrooms was R. Gordon Wasson, a vice president for J. P. Morgan bank and an amateur mycologist. In the summer of 1955, Wasson and his friend Allan Richardson, a photographer, traveled to Mexico and ingested psilocybin mushrooms at a remote location in the Mixeteco Mountains. In Mexico, these mushrooms are known as *teonanacatl*, or "flesh of the gods."[10]

In an article published in *Life* magazine in 1957, Wasson claimed that he and Richardson "were the first white men in recorded history to eat the divine mushrooms, which for centuries have been a secret of certain Indian peoples living far from the great world in southern Mexico."[11] Wasson's widely circulated article piqued the interest of those seeking to understand and push the envelope on human consciousness.

One such person was rising academic star Dr. Timothy Leary, a psychologist who had just gotten a position at Harvard University. At the end of his first year of teaching at Harvard, Leary traveled with other faculty to Cuernavaca, Mexico, to try his luck with the magic fungi. Six mushroom caps and four hours later, the forty-year-old Leary was transformed. "Like everyone else who has had the veil drawn," he would write, "I came back a changed man."[12] Beatnik hero and literary icon Neal Cassady considered psilocybin "the ultimate high."[13] Leary had given Cassady his first dose of the drug during a session in a New

York City apartment in the early 1960s. Cassady said the drug "combines the good sides of every other drug with none of the bad. . . . More mellow and cozy than heroin, but you don't nod out. . . . More alive and wired than with speed, but not jangly. It's got the blast of cocaine, but it lasted ten times longer. It's spacey like the best hashish, but also light and bouncy."[14]

Psilocybin mushrooms grow naturally all over Florida. In one of nature's ironies, they spring up out of cow patties. They can be picked right from the cow dung, dusted off, and consumed directly, or they may be stored, dried, made into tea, or combined with almost any food or beverage. According to research published in *JAMA Psychiatry* (formerly *Archives for General Psychiatry*), "clinical examinations of psilocybin have indicated that it is not hazardous to physical health."[15] For some who consume them, magic mushrooms can provide an extremely meaningful, even life-changing, experience. Terence McKenna refers to the mushroom experience as a "shamanic ecstasy" whereby an individual surrenders to "the mystery of being."[16] In his utopian novel *Island,* British writer Aldous Huxley (of *Brave New World* and *Doors of Perception* fame) describes how couples should consume mushrooms once a year to reestablish their union and work through any relational problems they may be having. The 1960s countercultural guru, chemist, and Grateful Dead sound engineer Owsley Stanley spoke for many when he claimed that psychedelic drugs like mushrooms "bring an understanding of the ecology of the planet and the interaction of all living things. That's one of the first things you become aware of when you take psychedelics—how everything is alive and everything depends on everything else."[17]

Ledbetter would have well understood the nature of such insights.[18] Psychedelic mushrooms were undergoing something of a revival in the late 1980s and early 1990s when he was an undergraduate, a trend likely related to twentieth- and twenty-fifth-anniversary celebrations of watershed events from the 1960s such as the Beatles' *Sergeant Pepper* album and the Woodstock music festival. As a writer for the *Florida Flambeau* declared in the summer of 1991, "People once again are boiling, steaming, and just plain ol' eating psilocybin mushrooms. People who by day are students, lawyers, nurses and state workers are leaving their tensions and pretensions behind and going with the hallucinogenic flow."[19]

Mushrooms were extraordinarily plentiful in Tallahassee in Ledbetter's day. In fact, it was hard to avoid them. An acquaintance of Ledbetter's was on a Leon County work crew one morning in the early 1990s, working off a petty drug charge by picking up trash along the highway. He remembers how strange it was looking through a fence into an adjacent field and seeing psilocybin mushrooms all over place, almost mocking him with their presence. Of course he didn't pick them. The possession of such contraband is highly illegal, and the penalties are severe, then as well as now. However, it is interesting to note that under Florida law (as determined by the 1978 case *Fiske v. Florida*) it is a crime to possess magic mushrooms only if it can be proven that the individual caught with them actually knew they contained psilocybin. There are, of course, many kinds of non-hallucinogenic mushrooms that also grow in Florida's temperate climate that people may pick without fear. The Florida Supreme Court apparently did not want innocent pickers caught up in the drug war dragnet. Tallahassee Police Department spokesperson Mark Meadows told the *Flambeau* that although people caught with psilocybin mushrooms could in theory be charged with a felony, it was rare for anyone to be prosecuted for more than trespassing. "Whenever (officers) get near people (they) throw them all down on the ground and the case is gone," Meadows said. "You can't get fingerprints off mushrooms."[20]

Leon County sheriff Larry Campbell, who has now worked in Florida law enforcement for over fifty years, knows this as well as any police officer. He says that of course you can still find psilocybin mushrooms all over Tallahassee and in the surrounding Leon County. Every spring and summer after heavy rains, Campbell says, he receives phone calls from farmers and ranchers complaining about trespassers. They report odd-looking people out in their fields, scaring the cows and knocking down fences. If you ever see people in the cow pastures having "a little picnic out there at midnight," you can bet they are looking for psychedelic mushrooms, Campbell says.[21]

The effects of ingesting mushrooms can be profound. According to British psychologists Sarah Riley and Graham Blackman, "Small amounts of mushrooms can produce subtle visual hallucinations and strange thoughts and feelings, high doses have the potential to produce open and closed eye visuals, feelings of time-dilation, belonging and connection, religious and spiritual awakening, extreme emotional responses, and intense feelings of wonder, connection, joy, and fear."[22] McKenna, one of the leading authorities on the subject, writes that "psilocybin intoxication is a rapture whose breadth and depth is the despair of prose. It is wholly Other and no less mysterious to us than it was to our mushroom-munching ancestors."[23] During the drug experience, "bizarre ideas, often hilariously funny, curious insights, some seeming almost godlike in their profundity, shards of memories and free-form hallucinations all clamor for attention."[24]

Today, long after the 1960s countercultural revolution, psychedelic mushrooms are increasingly being investigated for their therapeutic purposes. Dr. Roland Griffiths and his colleagues at Johns Hopkins are exploring the positive links between psilocybin use and personality structure. Their research posits an intriguing connection between psilocybin intake and personal openness and suggests that high doses of the substance can elevate moods and influence attitudes for more than year.[25] Fascinating research is also being conducted on psychedelic mushroom use in terminally ill patients as a way to help them cope with end-of-life concerns.[26]

Not all people respond positively to psychedelic mushrooms, however, and there is little research on long-term use. Negative effects can include dilated pupils, elevated heart rate, and "the experience of nausea, anxiety, panic, and/or being caught in a negative loop of thinking during intoxication."[27] Although a Norwegian research team recently found no link whatsoever between mushroom use and mental illness, many psychologists continue to believe that the ingestion of psychedelic mushrooms can lead to "the triggering of latent mental health problems."[28]

The psychedelic mushrooms were certainly out in force in April 1991. One evening near sundown, after two days of torrential rain, Marshall and his friends went mushroom hunting in a field about five miles outside Tallahassee. What they discovered amazed them—over four hundred psilocybin mushrooms growing up all over the field. After about an hour of foraging, the students had filled up two large trash bags with mushrooms. Even for some of the more experienced in the group, this was quite a haul. The students were giddy and ecstatic, and also quite nervous, given the felonious nature of their bounty. They got the mushrooms to the car and back to town. They went to a friend's apartment and spread them out on the bathroom tiles to dry.

Never had they seen so many mushrooms. A whole cadre of twenty-something FSU Seminoles tripped long and hard on those mushrooms that evening, carrying on throughout the night and into the early hours of the following day. Everyone in the group slept late, and upon waking in the afternoon, many decided to take the mushrooms again. On the third day, most of the group had begged off to resume their studies, but there was a committed core willing to go another round. By the sixth or seventh day, however, Marshall Ledbetter was all alone, and still taking the psychedelic mushrooms.

It was around this time that friends say Marshall started calling himself Raven and announced that he was embarking on a vision quest. Ledbetter declared his plan was to take psychedelic mushrooms every day for thirty consecutive days, ostensibly as an "experiment to churn his superior brain as fast and efficiently as a supercomputer."[29] His supply of mushrooms apparently ran out on day twenty-three. Despite not achieving his goal, this psychedelic vision quest was clearly a seminal experience for Marshall Ledbetter. Ledbetter had in effect removed the "reducing valve on his consciousness." He had opened the floodgates of sensory perception and was experiencing the "full force of the howling Tao." Marshall's mind had been converted into the "*paradis artificial*" of a vibrant hallucinatory dreamscape.[30]

Lemmy Kilmister, lead singer of Motörhead (one of Marshall's favorite rock bands), provides an account of his own drug use that offers us a window into what Marshall might have been experiencing for those twenty-three days. In reminiscing about his experiences taking LSD—a substance that shares a similar chemistry to psilocybin—in the late 1960s, Kilmister writes: "Real acid tripping, in those days, wasn't all groovy-like, peaceful shit. The first trip I took lasted eighteen hours, and I couldn't really see. All I saw were visions, not what was actually around me. Everything, every sound—you could snap your fingers and it would be like a kaleidoscope—doomph! Your eyes would just turn into noise-activated, coloured strobes. And all the time your mind felt like you were on a rollercoaster, sometimes slow at the approach to the top of each drop and then—wheeee! Your teeth would kind of sizzle, and if you started laughing, it was incredibly hard to stop."[31]

The experience was so much for the gruff rock and roller that even this heavy-metal tough guy issued stern warnings against the drug: "Acid is a dangerous drug . . . if you're complacent it will wake your ass up! If you were a little uneasy about yourself, you would either be catalyzed by it or you wouldn't show up again—you know, they'd take your tie and shoelaces away, and your belt, and put you in a room with no windows in it and lots of soft walls. A lot of people I know went to the basket-weavers' hotel on acid."[32]

Did Marshall Ledbetter check in at the "basket-weaver's hotel" after his twenty-three consecutive days of ingesting psychedelic mushrooms? Jasper Boehmke believes that this is indeed what happened to his old friend. Boehmke has no doubt that Marshall's prodigious drug use made him lose his mind. "After day ten or so he was not the same guy," he says. There was "an amazing difference" between who Marshall was before the vision quest and who he was afterward. Marshall was a "changed man." He had gone from being a brilliant, witty guy you wanted to be friends with to "the crazy guy you don't want to talk to." The old Marshall enjoyed "partying a lot, and having a good time." The new Marshall was "paranoid, conspiratorial, and hyper-opinionated."[33]

Iron Horse Adventures

He lives his life, he's living it fast
Don't try to hide, when the dice have been cast
He rides a whirlwind, that cuts to the bone
Loaded forever, and ferociously stoned.

Motörhead, "Iron Horse"

Many people encode themselves into lockdown. They only access one, or maybe two, spheres of human existence and have no idea of the vast data-stores existent, containing the sum of recorded human knowledge.

Marshall Ledbetter, "Tales of Psychoboy," October 1, 1996

Ledbetter continued partying into the middle of May, long after he had consumed all the magic mushrooms. He didn't show up for his final examinations. Marshall had once again flunked out of school. After Cawthon Hall closed its doors at the end of the term, Ledbetter had nowhere to go. He crashed where he could. He was unemployed and living off (what were then) the quite generous lending practices of America's largest financial institutions. It was in the early 1990s, when U.S. credit card companies first started aggressively marketing their wares to college students across the country. In practices that foreshadowed the Great Recession of 2008, Marshall Ledbetter had been approved for a number of large lines of credit without providing any proof of income. Andrew Arvesen remembers seeing Ledbetter in the FSU student union one day. He was heading to the campus post office with a stack of envelopes in his hand. "I'm applying for every card I can," Marshall told him.[1]

One day Ledbetter snapped his plastic on the counter to rent a silver, four-door Lincoln Town Car from Budget near Tallahassee Regional Airport. He needed the car to drive to Auburndale to see his family. He christened the vehicle "Iron Horse," a reference to the iconic song by Motörhead. During the trip, Marshall got in a serious car accident. According to Fritz Krawchuk, Ledbetter was not at fault. The car in front of him suddenly did a U-turn without warning, and he had no time to react. The driver of the other vehicle was seriously injured and, according to Krawchuk, was actually pronounced dead on the scene before being revived by an EMS crew. Ledbetter was relatively unscathed—just a little banged up. Marshall's face collided with the driver's-side airbag, which snapped his glasses across the bridge of his nose and left a nasty cut there.[2] The Town Car was totaled. But since Marshall had purchased the requisite insurance, Budget delivered a replacement vehicle of the same make and model without delay. Marshall dubbed the new vehicle "Iron Horse II."

Marshall's mother suggests that this is when the family first became quite concerned about their son. She says that the family was very worried when he came to visit them and that they tried to help him. They called around to different mental-health facilities in the area to see if they would take Marshall in. She had no luck. The cheapest available residential facility would have cost $5,000 per week (1990 dollars) for a minimum of six weeks to admit Marshall to their institution.[3] "Marshall's well-being was not ignored by his family," says Sharon. "We knew there was an issue, and we were trying to address the problem. We were trying to point him in the right direction. We were trying to find a place for him without bankrupting the family."[4]

Sharon thought that Marshall had no business driving around in a rental car in his state of mind. One day she got the rental contract and the keys to the Iron Horse II and called Budget to try to return the vehicle. She says the manager told her that Marshall had legally rented the car with a valid credit card and had purchased the requisite insurance. He said there was nothing they could do and that she should mind her own business.

Ledbetter left his family and drove the car back from Auburndale to Tallahassee. Then, in an apparent homage to Hunter S. Thompson's classic novel *Fear and Loathing in Las Vegas*, Marshall kept the keys and took off into the great unknown. He drove the Iron Horse II all over the Southeast for another week or so. Marshall had a couple of other ne'er-do-wells—referred to mockingly by his closer friends as the "Sycophants"—with him as he cruised around, taking advantage of Ledbetter's naïveté and apparent largesse.[5] They were living completely off credit cards and credit card checks, stopping mainly for provisions at liquor stores and gas stations. During one break in the madness, Marshall phoned his old Landis Hall buddy Bradley Pepperman[6] in Tallahassee. He told him he was in Georgia flat broke and needed money. Marshall asked his friend to wire him some cash. Pepperman refused. Somehow, Marshall and his crew made it back to Tallahassee. Since he didn't have anywhere to stay, Ledbetter decided to live out of the rental car, declaring it "liberated" from Budget. The trunk of the vehicle was stuffed with Ledbetter's belongings and other items.

Jonathan Lammers says that it was when he saw the "hundreds of dollars' worth of cheap plastic supermarket toys" in the trunk of Ledbetter's car that he knew a "switch had been flipped" in Marshall's brain.[7] "Marshall might do odd stuff now and then, but you could always see the viewpoint behind it. These random purchases were not in character for him. . . . It just seemed dumb and purposeless," he says.[8] There was also graffiti all over the car. Marshall had scrawled two political slogans on the vehicle in a black permanent marker, altering the vehicle's aesthetic considerably. On the side of the car, Marshall had written in large letters: "United States of Genocide." On the trunk, he wrote "10^5 Dead Iraqi Children. Bush. He Ain't No Wimp."

The rest of the car was in pretty bad shape too. Eric Witherspoon recalls seeing Ledbetter's car one day with "dents and spray paint all over it." He said it looked like it "had run into something or had something run into it."[9] For his part, Marshall was lucky get back to Tallahassee in one piece. Displaying such bizarre sloganeering and carousing all over rural north Florida and southern Georgia had not been prudent. Although much of Leon County is known as being fairly liberal, its surrounding counties are certainly not so. Folks in those parts don't take kindly to wild rhetorical jousts, especially coming from dirty, wild-eyed hippies driving a Lincoln.

On the evening of May 28, 1991, Marshall was stopped by an officer with the Tallahassee Police Department while driving the Iron Horse II through town. Earlier in the day he had written a letter to his credit card companies telling them that he was under no obligation to live up to the terms of his credit card agreement.[10] They should stop bothering him, Ledbetter told them; he wasn't going to pay.

Ledbetter was pulled over when a patrol officer saw him driving with his high beams on in heavy traffic in downtown Tallahassee, not too far from the capitol building. In collecting Marshall's paperwork, the officer found Marshall to be slurring his words and smelling of alcohol. Ledbetter was ordered to take a field sobriety test. He failed all six exercises. After he refused to take the breathalyzer test, Marshall was arrested and charged with driving under the influence. The officer ran the license plate on the vehicle and found that it belonged not to a 1991 Lincoln but a 1973 Mercedes.[11] Ledbetter was written a ticket for that offense, too. Marshall's belongings were confiscated. These included large plastic garbage bags filled with magazines, toys, papers, and clothing, three boxes of books (including five overdue items from Strozier Library), seven Florida State keys, and a VHS camcorder.[12]

All of this was happening while Marshall's younger siblings, Arlen and Carla, were graduating from high school. It was a very busy time for the family. Later in the week, Marshall's parents drove to Tallahassee to try to see Marshall and bring him back home. When they got to the jail, however, they found, much to their surprise, that their son had been released and he was no longer in police custody. Marshall's personal items would be signed over to his mother on May 31. Sharon and her husband were "upset, frustrated and concerned" about what was happening to Marshall, and they looked all over Tallahassee trying to find him. Apparently, though, Marshall was working hard not to be found. Eventually, they gave up. "We had no way to find him. We didn't know where he was," says Sharon. They drove to Strozier Library to return the overdue books and headed back to Auburndale. They had driven over five hundred miles without seeing or communicating with Marshall.

When they got home there was a call from the manager at Budget. It was the same man whom Sharon had spoken with earlier when she was trying to return the Town Car without Marshall's permission. Although he had been quite short with her earlier when he told her she had no right to meddle in her son's affairs, now the manager wanted to speak to her about all the damage Marshall had done to the vehicle. The manager wanted the Ledbetters to pay for the damage. Ledbetter told the man that it was none of their business and hung up.

It appears that Marshall had spent only two days behind bars in Leon County Detention Center before being released on his own recognizance. His DUI charges would be pending. Since Marshall had refused to take the breathalyzer test during the traffic stop, his license was suspended for a year. He hoofed it from the jail back into town. A friend recognized him along the side of the road and picked him up. He had just bought a twelve-pack of beer and offered one to Marshall, who was thirsty after a week in lockup. They drank beer together and then went to the Cow Haus, a popular musical venue then on Lake Bradford Road on the south end of Tallahassee. Marshall was happy to be reunited with his friends. He drank more beer and chatted about his jailhouse experience. Fritz Krawchuk remembers that Marshall was "a little bit proud of being in the jail; like a hardened criminal."[13] Marshall gave his friends an update on his most recent entrepreneurial schemes, his plans of broadcasting Public Enemy videos into outer space, and how—through his consumption of so much psilocybin—he had managed to rewire his entire nervous system.[14] A few days later, Marshall would go to the animal testing laboratory in the Biomedical Research Facility at Florida State and ask the researchers—who normally study hamsters and voles—to run diagnostics on him instead.[15]

Despite Marshall's apparent good cheer, an objective assessment would indicate that it had been a tough semester for the young man. Over the last few weeks, Ledbetter had dropped out of school, had been in a car accident, and had been charged with DUI. He was broke and was living in a stolen rental car with fake tags. People started to wonder if Marshall had slipped off the deep end. His friends had watched with a mixture of pity, horror, and fascination as Marshall put his body through extraordinary feats of intoxication, but now they were beginning to worry. A close female friend of Marshall's would later tell the *Orlando Sentinel*, "He's just had a lot of problems."[16] In a television interview, she elaborated: "It was just Marshall's charm to be, I don't know . . . weird . . . to be different. But it's just gotten a lot worse. It's gone from . . . let's run around a pool at four in the morning to things that are more serious."[17]

Gregory Cohen remembers Marshall's friends debating whether they should lock Marshall in a room for a while so he could pull himself together.[18] Jonathan Lammers admits that the subject arose "when Marshall's behavior grew increasingly erratic." The group was not "seriously considering locking him in a room," but Marshall's "behavior had grown uncomfortably strange even for us."[19] The group of students started to have some serious conversations about committing their friend Marshall to a psychiatric hospital.

The 1971 Florida Mental Health Bill, generally referred to as the "Baker Act," allows Florida residents to be involuntarily institutionalized for up to seventy-two hours if it is thought they have a mental illness and are a danger to themselves or others. Some friends thought Ledbetter met these criteria and argued that such intervention was the sensible course of action. Marshall was becoming increasingly unstable, and it might only be a matter of time before something terrible happened. Better to "Baker Act" him now than to regret not doing so later. But others in the group thought this was an overreaction and objected on libertarian grounds. To them, Marshall's behavior, though obnoxious and perhaps even offensive, didn't warrant involuntary commitment to a psychiatric hospital. Though he was clearly behaving strangely, Marshall hadn't in fact hurt himself or anyone else. Perhaps all the peculiarities of his behavior could simply be attributed to all his drinking and drug use.

At the end of the day, no one could make a decision. It was almost the end of the semester, and when it came down to it, having Marshall committed just seemed like too much of a hassle. "Let the experiment continue" was the uneasy consensus. Bradley Pepperman remembers: "Talk of Baker Acting Marshall started pretty early during the vision-quest. . . . But resorting to violence wasn't appealing to any of us, and the thought of turning a friend in to the authorities was kind of appalling given how little any of us trusted those authorities during this period. Most of us probably recited the words to the Suicidal Tendencies' 'Institutionalized' regularly."[20]

Ledbetter's friends decided to watch and wait. Fritz Krawchuk remembers that during "that last week or so, Marshall had become kind of a bum."[21] Ledbetter declared he would no longer use "the white man's soap."[22] Arvesen describes the Marshall of that moment as "the guy who was out of his head on psychedelics and needed a shower."[23] Eric Witherspoon remembers seeing Marshall at a party and hardly recognizing his old friend: "He was doing stuff I didn't want to be a part of. And I didn't even want to know what it was."[24] Ledbetter was increasingly asking his friends for food, handouts, and a place to sleep (since his car by this point had been impounded). Marshall was writing "scores of bad checks for anything and everything."[25] He could be observed now more regularly bending an ear to and talking to homeless people, and buying groceries for them at Publix.

Friend Chris Boose remembers that "Marshall didn't care what he said" to anybody. Even though his initial stash had run out, he soon found access to even more mushrooms. Boose says it seems Ledbetter was taking mushrooms "at least every other day." He "didn't sleep" and was "always, always, tripping."[26] Largely because of such behavior, many of his friends stopped hanging around him as much. Listeners who didn't respond favorably to Marshall's rants were accused of being sellouts or dupes. For the ones who still paid attention, it seemed to be the same old spiel. To borrow a quote from Hunter S. Thompson, Marshall had descended into "a form of surly madness so wrong and rotten that only the Wretched and the Scum of the Earth," could understand it.[27]

Ledbetter was starting to become a bit of a nuisance. One morning in early June he paid a visit to the WVFS radio station on the fourth floor of the Diffenbaugh Building on FSU campus. As former WFVS DJ Lindee Morgan remembers, "I was arriving at the station for a weekday 6 a.m. shift," and Marshall "was actually already there . . . had been there a few minutes." The midnight-to-6 a.m. DJ "had her dog with her . . . a German shepherd named Haggis. Marshall had mushrooms and was offering them up. At one point [the DJ] thought her dog was eating some of the mushrooms. She had a mini-freak-out until she realized he was munching on something else. I asked Marshall to leave shortly after that."[28] Marshall did not put up any resistance and went on his way. "From what I remember he was sort of oblivious," Morgan says. "He said he'd been tripping for a few weeks straight."

Bert Peppe, Ledbetter's friend and chess partner, tried to bring Marshall back from the edge. "What the fuck are you doing?" demanded Peppe one day, trying to talk some sense into his good friend. It was Ledbetter's twenty-second birthday, and Peppe was buying him another meal at the McDonald's on Tennessee Street. "You don't even have the money to buy yourself a McLean sandwich, Marshall," he said. "You're all talk, talk, talk. When are you going to get off your ass and do something?" The chastened Marshall turned glum. He accused Peppe of being a traitor and told him he could no longer listen to the Sex Pistols. "One day my voice will mock you from the abyss," Ledbetter griped.[29]

Yet the pep talk seems to have had its intended effect. Later that afternoon, Ledbetter was listening to WFSU, Tallahassee's public radio station. He discovered that Governor Lawton Chiles would be on the air and taking questions from callers. Marshall decided to phone one in:

> Host (Jo Miglino): Another call from Tallahassee right now. Marshall is on the line with a question about university tuition.
> Marshall: Hello.
> Miglino: [Pause] Yes, you're on the line, Marshall. Go ahead with your question.
> Marshall: Uh, yeah, it's basically concerning the tuition situation like in the State University System. As students every year we face increased tuition and less and less class space and so forth, but I'm quite sure that people out there familiar with the State University System know about this already. What I wanted to do was quite possibly throw out a few concepts at you and just get your opinion on the feasibility of this.
> Miglino: Well, real quickly, real quickly.
> Marshall: Yeah, real quickly. I'm going as fast as I can.

Miglino: Uh, okay.

Marshall: It's a situation where the faculty in our State University System are some of the most intelligent people that I have ever met on this earth. And here we are, sitting on a bunch of cyber super computers and so forth and we could be generating media in terms of uh, virtual reality computer programs, gaming programs, rap albums, whatever, and marketing this. . . . This could basically pay for the entire State University System.

Miglino: Marshall . . .

Marshall: Hello?

Miglino: Okay, I'm going to ask you real quick, do you want the governor's thoughts on university tuition and where it stands right now?

Marshall: Uh, yeah, I mean am I like going even get a chance to talk to him personally or is this sort of a secondhand thing?

Miglino: Yeah, he's right here, ask him a question.

Marshall: Yeah, what I was wondering is . . . I mean, if you don't think this will work, all I ask is that you go and check out Walter Tschinkel lecturing on insects for a couple of hours. This guy is unbelievable. If you had like three hours with a Walter Tschinkel rapping about insects, I mean you could take all the bass lines and beats and it would be the click beetles, like basically all the flora and fauna from Tallahassee and so forth. I'm quite sure you could sell this at like twenty bucks a pop and move fifty million albums, that would be a billion dollars right there and just from one three-hour lecture from one man in one department in one subject.

Miglino: OK, thanks a lot, thanks a lot. What do you think about that?

Lawton Chiles: [*Chuckles*] It sounds like a good business that you and I ought to get into. If that kind of profit can be generated, then come see me and let's put together something.[30]

Chiles asked a rhetorical follow-up question. "How do we commercialize some of that?" The governor then added: "I think you've got some very, very good thoughts and we're trying to work in that regard."[31]

Four days and one whisky bottle later, Marshall did in a sense did go and see the Florida governor to "put together something." His timing and coordinates were slightly skewed, though. Instead of heading to the governor's office, Marshall wound up in the Sergeant at Arms suite, and Lawton Chiles was still in bed.

A Late Night at the Hogly

ARE YOU ABNORMAL? THEN YOU ARE PROBABLY BETTER
THAN MOST PEOPLE. YES! YOUR KIND SHALL TRIUMPH!
SUPERIOR MUTANTS! REPENT! QUIT YOUR JOB! SLACK
OFF!

The Book of the SubGenius

I got the image of Bob Dobbs, I sat down, wrote my note of
demands, visited some friends, and went on to the capitol.

**Marshall Ledbetter in Dr. William Spence, "Court-Ordered
Psychological Evaluation," July 2, 1991**

It was not the first time Marshall Ledbetter had been at the Hogly
Wogly in the early hours of the morning. In fact, it was one of his
regular hangouts. A three-minute walk from Landis Hall, Ledbetter's
old dormitory, the Hogly was one of those quintessential outposts of
American convenience. It consisted of a functioning gas station with
all the amenities of a convenience store, plus limited alcoholic beverage service of beer and wine, red faux leather bar and booth sitting,
and a grill menu. The place was open around the clock. After a night
of partying, ranting, or just hanging out with friends, Marshall would
wander around the campus and then go to the Hogly. He would harass
his friend and old roommate Chris Boose, who worked the graveyard
shift as bartender and clerk. The Hogly was a useful way station for the
aspiring rap artist and producer. Given their friendship, Boose usually tolerated Marshall and his antics. If nothing else, Marshall's visits
helped pass the time and kept him from falling asleep.

Marshall had been keeping odd hours since he had been released
from jail, staying up most of the night while sleeping away the days on

the sofas of accommodating friends. After spending two nights in jail, Ledbetter had stayed about a week at John Griffin's place (another old friend from Landis Hall). He then moved on to live with Steven Profit, aka Steven the Provocative and Pure, an integral member of the Monarchy Party's "Royal Family."[1] Profit had an apartment at 543 West Park Avenue, on the space that is now a parking lot behind Bill's Bookstore.

Marshall had awoken that Thursday morning in yet another hungover state. He spent most of the day listening to music and rehydrating himself at Profit's apartment. On an existential level, Ledbetter must have sensed that he was going round the bend and would have been struggling to keep it together. Some of his comrades had been starting to get annoyed with him, and in an attempt at goodwill one evening he took them out to dinner. Ledbetter had spent a fortune with money he didn't have at the Asian Wok, a favorite Chinese restaurant on Tennessee Street. They group ran up a two-hundred-dollar tab of assorted food and cocktails. Marshall settled up by paying with another credit card check, much to the disapproval of the proprietor.[2]

It had been a riotous evening, with Marshall and his friends basically taking over the place. This irritated some of the other customers. Ledbetter eventually sent a bottle of wine as an apology to a disgruntled gentleman and his wife. As sunset burned through the bamboo fringes of the window framing Tennessee Street, the man refused the wine, and then, more vehemently, the very shirt off Marshall's back, which had been removed as riposte to the other's affront. Luckily, things didn't get ugly.[3]

And now here stood Marshall Robin Ledbetter Jr. at the Hogly Wogly chatting with his good buddy Chris Boose. It was about 2:15 a.m. on June 14, 1991, four days after Ledbetter's twenty-second birthday. The night was a cool sixty-five degrees. A waxing crescent moon hung in the sky. There had been a small party earlier that evening at Profit's apartment, the engine of which was a liter of Jack Daniels. After the party wound down, only Marshall and his host were left. Recalling his earlier conversation with Governor Lawton Chiles and perhaps wanting to get out of Profit's hair for a while, Marshall announced: "I'm gonna go talk to the governor some more."[4] He grabbed the whisky bottle and took off. In an odd move, he also scooped up Profit's driver's license as he headed out the door. It is unclear why he did this. Ledbetter would have surrendered his own driver's license to the police when he refused to take the breathalyzer test during his DUI stop. It is possible that Marshall just wanted to have some sort of identification on him, in order to buy beer, perhaps. But it is not evident how his friend's ID would have helped. Marshall was white and stood five foot eleven. Profit is a black man and two inches shorter.

Around midnight, while drifting along the streets of Tallahassee, Marshall had a vision that would forever change his life. In his words, he suddenly "got the image of Bob Dobbs."[5] Although further details of just how the SubGenius deity—haircut, pipe, and everything—appeared to Marshall Ledbetter at this particular moment in time are unknown to the author and most likely forever lost to history, the apparition served as a stimulus to action. This was the sign Marshall had been waiting for. Something big was about to happen. But first he had to develop his plan of attack.

Boose remembers that night well. He says Marshall came in to the Hogly Wogly holding a bottle of "rot gut [and] chugging from a bottle of tequila if I remember correctly."[6] After about a half an hour of conversation, Boose says, Marshall handed him a note with some odd writing on it. Ledbetter then bade his friend goodnight and left the store. On his way out, Ledbetter bumped into their mutual friend John Griffin, with whom he had been staying the week before, and who lived just round the corner. Some additional banter ensued with Griffin and Boose. After a couple of minutes, Marshall said to them both: "You know what? I've had enough. I'm going to take over the capitol."[7] He marched out the door and vanished into the night.

Boose and Griffin didn't take Marshall's declaration very seriously. Griffin remembers: "Chris and I looked at each other. Chris said something along the lines of 'OK, right. Whatever.' We went back to talking and looking at titty mags."[8] Marshall's discourse had been rather fantastical lately, and this remark just seemed like business as usual. Marshall's friends never expected him to make good on his threat. The next day, Griffin would tell the *Orlando Sentinel* that Marshall "talks constantly. You have to tune him out sometimes."[9]

Capitol Showdown

This was a declaration of war on the present day power
structure of this planet. . . . I was doing my best to invite a
world revolution.

**Marshall Ledbetter in Dr. William Spence, "Court-Ordered
Psychological Evaluation," July 2, 1991**

There is a time when the operation of the machine becomes
so odious, makes you so sick at heart, that you can't take
part; you can't even passively take part, and you've got to
put your bodies upon the gears and upon the wheels, upon
the levers, upon all the apparatus, and you've got to make it
stop. And you've got to indicate to the people who run it, to
the people who own it, that unless you're free, the machine
will be prevented from working at all!

Mario Savio, "Sproul Hall Steps, December 2, 1964"

Marshall left the Hogly Wogly and headed east toward the State Capitol Building. For readers who may be unfamiliar with Tallahassee, the
state of Florida actually has two capitol buildings, one known as the
"old" capitol, and the other the "new" capitol. The former, the historic
capitol building, is a quaint, domed structure at the corner of Monroe
Street and Apalachee Parkway. It was built in 1845, underwent serious renovation in 1902, and served "as the core of Florida's Capitol
despite numerous additions," until 1978.[1] Today, the historic capitol
houses a museum and bookshop. The portico on the front of the building displays the Great Seal of Florida, adopted in 1868, which depicts
"a view of the sun's rays over a high land in the distance, a cocoa tree,
a steamboat on water, and an Indian female scattering flowers in the
foreground."[2] The new capitol, completed in 1978, is now the real house

of power in the state. It sits directly behind and literally towers over the older building. NPR commentator and Floridian Diane Roberts tells us that after the new capitol was built, Governor Reubin Askew targeted the old capitol for demolition. He thought it "was a relic of the Old South; slaves had been sold from its wide steps." In response, the Garden Club, the Historical Society, and the Daughters of the Confederacy mobilized resistance, even threatening "to throw themselves in front of the bulldozers" to save the building.[3]

The new capitol was designed by famed American modernist architect Edward Durell Stone (1902–78) and would be one of his last major projects. Stone built the capitol to represent the state in the midst of "an age of fast-moving, sometimes unpredictable and even frightening events."[4] In the late 1970s the size of the structure was impressive: twenty-two stories and a height of 307 feet. At the time it was built, it was the tallest building between Jacksonville and New Orleans.[5] The new Florida capitol structure also featured two large domes five stories off the ground on either side of the monolith, resulting in what might be considered a textbook example of phallocentric architecture. In the late 1970s, the $45 million building was on the cutting edge of architecture and became the dominant force on the Tallahassee skyline. When it was finished, the capitol complex had more than a thousand rooms and a million square feet.[6] Everything was state of the art. The building had a robust security system operated by computers and electronic sensors.[7] Italian marble adorned the walls on the plaza Level, and a sophisticated heating system that utilized "heat from human bodies, lights and other electrical devices" warmed the building.[8]

Ledbetter arrived at the capitol building a little after 3:00 a.m. He was wearing acid-washed shorts, flip-flops, and a faded purple tie-dyed Jimi Hendrix T-shirt. He surveyed the scene and weighed the advantages and disadvantages of various entry points into the building. He noticed a Capitol Police officer on patrol but evaded her view. He waited for the right time to act.

About an hour later, Ledbetter wrapped a towel around the empty bottle of whisky he had been carrying and approached a doorway. He was on the south side (Adams Street) of the plaza level. He took a roll of masking tape from his pocket and affixed the tape in strips on

The Florida capitol buildings seen from Apalachee Parkway, looking west toward Tallahassee. The new capitol is the dominant feature on the Tallahassee skyline, dwarfing the historic capitol in front of it. Designed by Edward Durrell Stone, the new capitol is a particularly impressive example of phallocentric architecture. Photo courtesy of Jason Flom.

the door to muffle the noise of glass breaking. Marshall hit the towel-wrapped bottle hard against the glass. The window didn't break. Marshall hit it again. It still didn't break. He reconsidered his technique. This time, Marshall tapped on the glass gently, gradually at first with light taps and increasing the force with each swing. He hit the glass six or seven more times. On the final blow, the window shattered. It was 4:04 a.m.

Strangely, no security alert was triggered when Marshall smashed the window. No lights were tripped, no alarms sounded, no automated phone calls were dialed to the police. No black helicopters swept down on Ledbetter from over the rooftops. Incredibly, despite the new capitol building's technological wizardry, no sensors had been embedded in the building's glass doors. Even though Ledbetter had struck a major blow to its defenses, the capitol's computerized alarm system still registered the building as secure.

Marshall made his way inside and took a look around. He left one note for police near the entrance and another down the hall. The first note read: "It would be advisable to leave the building and contact your superiors. There is a note on front of the columns @ the front entrance. Tell your fellow officers no harm will come to them if they do not penetrate the confines of the edifice." It was signed "Smoking Raven in the Eye of the Great Storm." Marshall made his way to the main lobby and got on an elevator. He rode it up and down for a while before getting worried he might be under surveillance, and so he stepped off.

At around 4:15 Marshall went to use pay phone on the fifth floor. He dialed 911. He told the dispatcher, "The Capitol building is occupied and you will find a note by the door."[9] The operator alerted Tallahassee Police Department personnel in the area. Two officers and a K-9 dog were sent to investigate. When they got to the capitol, however, "patrol officers were unable to find the broken door and assumed the report was false."[10] The officers left the premises. It was now about 5:00 a.m. Ledbetter had been amped for a showdown with the police, yet the opposition wasn't showing up. This must have been maddening for him. Here he was trying to make his stand for freedom, justice, and liberty, and he was getting punked. Where the hell was everybody?

It would be advisable
to leave the building
and contact your
superiors.
There is a note on the
front of one of the
columns @ the front
entrance. Tell your
fellow officers no harm
will come to them if
they do not penetrate
the confines of the
edifice.

Smoking Raven in
the Eye of the
Great Storm

The first note Marshall Ledbetter left
for police during his occupation of the
capitol building on June 14, 1991.

Marshall once again had the capitol building all to himself. He
cruised around the empty floors and corridors. His shorts and flip-
flops must have been holding him back, so he took them off. He found
himself in front of room 403, the Office of the Sergeant at Arms (for
the Florida Senate). The signage on the door appealed to Ledbetter.
It was vaguely militaristic, just like his own name. He tried the door,
which to his surprise was open. Apparently, a painting crew had left it
unlocked the previous evening.[11] Marshall walked in and made himself
at home.

Given the title of the office, Ledbetter might have been expecting to
find considerable firepower inside the suite. He would be disappointed.
Like his counterpart in the Florida House, the main job of the Sergeant
at Arms for the Senate is to keep the wheels of Florida governance
running smoothly. According to the *Associated Press*, "The Sergeant is,

officially, in charge of purchasing supplies and seeing to the security of the Senate. Unofficially, the clerks and sergeants in both the House and Senate ensure their own re-elections every two years by meeting—anticipating—the creature comforts of 160 busy, demanding, ambitious people with all the human foibles that the rest of us enjoy."[12]

Ledbetter looked around the suite. There were two administrative offices and a small kitchen. Marshall decided to barricade the entrance. He shoved a leather couch behind the two large wooden doors to stop them from opening. Marshall went into the office of Wayne Todd, the actual sergeant at arms, and rooted around. He uncovered a box of Hav-a-Tampa cigars and a sizable stash of liquor bottles. Ledbetter removed the tops from all the liquor bottles.[13] He went back into the other room and rifled through the desk of Todd's office assistant, Julie Anderson. He ate her Captain's Wafers and made coffee in the kitchen. He knocked over some of Anderson's treasured African violets growing on the windowsill.[14] Marshall went back to Todd's office. He poured himself a glass of bourbon, lit a cigar, and waited for the police.

The State Responds

My bottom line is they are my enemy, all those in power
who speak lies. . . . What I did was right.

**Marshall Ledbetter in Dr. William Spence, "Court-Ordered
Psychological Evaluation," July 2, 1991**

Woop-woop!
That's the sound of da police!
Woop-woop!
That's the sound of the beast!

KRS-One, "Sound of Da Police"

Sergeant at Arms Wayne Todd was fishing when he heard the news. He
was on his boat near Carrabelle, a small coastal retirement community
southwest of Tallahassee, when the Coast Guard found him. Todd was
informed that earlier that morning someone had broken into and was
presently occupying the State Capitol Building in Tallahassee. The details were sketchy, but it was thought the intruder might have hostages
and perhaps even a bomb.

Todd got to his car and headed back to Tallahassee. He called the
State Highway Patrol to let them know he was driving back to town
very quickly and needed the roads cleared.[1] Usually for Todd this would
have been a pleasant, meandering drive along the Florida coast, with
scenic views of the Gulf of Mexico, crumbling seafood restaurants,
trailer parks draped in moss, and thousands of acres of pine forest.
Today all of this would be distant from his mind, and he made the drive
to Tallahassee in record time. It was about 8:00 a.m.

Todd's rapid response was entirely appropriate. A big part of his
job as sergeant at arms was to maintain order, the very opposite of

what was occurring that very minute. And to makes matters worse, not only was this peculiar break-in happening on his day off, but the intruder had somehow managed to gain entry to and was barricaded inside Todd's very own office. The event would be memorialized as the most serious security breach to occur during his thirty-year career at the capitol.[2]

Leon County undersheriff Larry Campbell had put out the call to locate the sergeant at arms. Campbell had a degree in criminology from Florida State and had gotten his start in law enforcement in 1961 working at the Leon County jail.[3] Forty-five years later he became Leon County sheriff, a post he holds to the present day, even as he battles cancer.[4] Sheriff Campbell has the sort gravelly voice you might expect from someone who has spent much of his life smoking cigarettes and drinking high-test police coffee. Think Colonel Jack Ripper from *Dr. Strangelove* but with a southern accent.

"We remember him," says Campbell. "That boy, he was a character."[5] Campbell says he was first informed about a possible intruder by the Capitol Police at about 7:30 a.m. Officers William Hartsfield and Jesse Lovett had been alerted to the incident when Ruby Dennis could not gain access to the Sergeant at Arms suite on the fourth floor of the capitol building. They responded to the scene. As Hartsfield and Lovett considered their options outside the barricaded door, they heard an unfamiliar voice over the secure channel on the radio.

"Call your dogs off," it crackled.[6] It was Marshall Ledbetter, using one of the police radios he had found inside the suite.

Hartsfield and Lovett needed backup. A call was put out to Campbell at the sheriff's office, who quickly took command of the situation. He ordered a more careful search of the building. On this sweep, the police found not only the first note Ledbetter had left for them but a more detailed list of demands as well. This note read:

BLACK WAMPUM + RED STICKS
(crackle, hiss!) 'Sarge, we got a hostage situation . . . '
Before taking any action it would be well to ascertain the quality of your opposition. Though it pains me to follow SOP, here are my demands at this point:

1 Gumby's 20 incher veggie w/extra jalapenos
1 Case of Asahi Dry
1 Carton of Lucky Strikes (filtered)
The contents of the Iron Horse I liberated from Budget
1 oz of Indica
1 CNN news crew (within the hour)
1 police band scanner
666 Dunkin Donuts for my fine friends in the TPD, FSUPD, and LCSD.
100$ worth of Chinese food. Check with John @ the Asian Wok for details
These will be delivered by anyone in the upper echelon of the Monarchy Party unless you can locate John Griffin or his roomie Ian.
I also wish to speak with Timothy Leary, Debbie Harlow, Lemmy, Jello and Ice Cube, for starters. Also Flavor Flav. Also the leadership of AIM. It would not be advisable to enter the building as you have no hard data concerning the # of hostiles and their weaponry.

At the bottom of the note were the following words:

Annihilate
Conditioning
Integrate
Data

In the center of the page, Marshall had drawn a picture of a raven smoking a cigarette, encircled by a ring of smoke. Beneath the drawing were the letters AWO in large, block letters.

Law enforcement went to work deciphering this important clue. Campbell assumed he was dealing with some sort of terrorist attack. He put a tactical response together, coordinating with different law-enforcement agencies and their personnel. Within an hour, "dozens of police sharpshooters, hostage negotiators, K-9 units and firefighters swarmed the Capitol complex."[7] Officers secured the third, fourth, and fifth floors of the building.[8] Snipers were placed on rooftops around

BLACK WAMPUM + RED STICKS

(crackle, hiss!) 'So'rge, we got a hostage situation...'

Before taking any action it would be well to ascertain the quality of your opposition. Though it pains me to follow SOP, here are my demands at this point:

- 1 Gumby's 20 incher veggie w/ extra jalpenos
- 1 Case of Asahi Dry
- 1 Carton Lucky Strikes (filtered)
- The contents of the Iron Horse I liberated from Budget.
- 1 oz of indica
- 1 CNN news crew (within an hour.)
- 1 police band scanner
- 666 Dunkin Donuts for my fine friends in the TPD, FSUPD, and LCSD
- 100$ worth of Chinese food. Check w/ John @ the Asian Wok for details

These will be delivered by anyone in the upper echelon of the Monarchy party unless you can locate John Griffin or his roomie Ian. I also wish to speak with Timothy Leary, Debbie Harlow, Lemmy, Jello, and Ice Cube, for starters. Also Flavor Flav. Also the leadership of AIM. It would not be advisable to enter the building as you have no hard data concerning the # of hostiles and their weaponry.

ANNIHILATE
CONDITIONING
INTEGRATE
DATA

AWO

The list of demands that Marshall Ledbetter left for police during his occupation of the capitol, titled "Black Wampum + Red Sticks."

the capitol courtyard. A SWAT team was placed in position outside the Sergeant at Arms suite, with guns trained on the doorway of room 403.

Campbell selected Sergeant Gilda Strickland as his hostage nego-tiator. She was one of four or five officers on the Leon County Sheriff Office staff whom Campbell would ask to help in hostage-negotiation situations like this. He had recently hired Strickland away from Florida State University's Campus Police.[9] She was in her twenties, with brown hair and a gentle southern accent.[10]

In the shards of glass near Ledbetter's first note, police came across Steven Profit's driver's license. They beat a hasty path to the address on the card. Profit must have been taken completely by surprise when the police banged on his door that morning.[11] He would have had no idea what his driver's license was doing at the capitol. Then it would have dawned on him who was to blame.

Profit let the deputies in. They combed through Ledbetter's belong-ings. They were alarmed to find a well-worn copy of the *Anarchist Cook-book* among his possessions. This countercultural tome, first published in 1971, was considered required reading for many rabble-rousing col-lege students in the latter part of the twentieth century. Most people never took the book very seriously, and if it was used for anything, it was mainly as an announcement of attempted hipness or pseudo-radicalism. Some of the more conspiratorially minded claimed the CIA itself was behind the publication, trying to get all the hippies and other countercultural types to poison each other or blow themselves up.

For the Leon County sheriff deputies working the case that day, the discovery of the *Anarchist Cookbook* was highly distressing. Campbell says that normally his officers would not be concerned with an alleged suspect's reading habits, but in this case the *Anarchist Cookbook* had been quite seriously thumbed, "dog-eared to the nth degree."[12] The un-settling possibility dawned on Campbell that "this guy knows how to make bombs."[13] This was particularly worrying, because oxygen tanks were stored in the Sergeant at Arms suite, kept on hand for medical emergencies. If those tanks exploded, things could get messy indeed. Campbell called the Tallahassee Fire Department, told them what was going on, and asked them to hurry over to the capitol. Together with all the police, press, and rubberneckers, they prepared for the worst.

Freelance reporter Mike Vasilinda of the Tallahassee-based Capitol News Service first learned of the break-in at the capitol a little after 8:00 a.m. Dan Bradley, assignment editor at WFLA in Tampa, had telephoned Vasilinda regarding an AP urgent notice about someone taking over the capitol building in Tallahassee.[14] Bradley told Vasilinda to "get up there, get the story [and] get it on television."[15] Vasilinda rushed to the capitol complex and joined a cadre of other reporters in the courtyard.

At about 8:30, Campbell, who was now acting as incident commander, briefed the assembled press corps. He was flanked by James McPherson, director of the Capitol Police force. It was clear the two men were taking the break-in very seriously. Campbell relayed the information he had about the situation. Someone had broken into the capitol in the middle of the night and was now occupying the Sergeant at Arms suite. Police had "found some notes at various places around the capitol." Campbell said the notes were "fairly incoherent" and contained "demands of no great consequence . . . donuts, liquor, some marijuana, things like that."[16]

Yet Campbell also said that "the notes indicate the possibility of hostages." He said, "The subject has a police-type radio and has communicated with law enforcement on one occasion. We know he is listening to our transmissions."[17] Campbell expressed concern about the field of view the capitol intruder might have from the window of the office suite. Campbell said his men had already cleared areas on the ground most vulnerable to a possible shot from the window. His team was developing a "tactical plan to see what sort of operation we will undertake," he said. They were "fixing to start a hostage negotiation process" and were about to "set up telephonic communications with him."[18]

At this point in their response, the police assumed Ledbetter had weapons. Campbell said, "He indicates he is armed." In a reference to the whisky bottle that Marshall had used to smash his way in to the building, Campbell said the intruder "left at least one diversionary-type device that was supposed to represent a bomb but was apparently not an activated type of weapon."[19] A reporter asked about the demands letter. "It is an incoherent note," Campbell replied. "He talks about how he represents some group whose acronym is ACID. . . . He's talking about AIM, several groups that we haven't even heard of. . . . We're running intelligence on them right now."[20]

Marshall's friends gathered together as they heard the news on the radio, television, or by word of mouth. Deon Gondron and Bert Peppe just happened to be getting ready for a canoe trip on the Wacissa River. They were heading out of town in Deon's pickup truck, listening to the public radio station, WFSU. A news alert told them a college student had taken over the capitol and had issued a strange list of demands. They knew instantly it was Marshall. They turned the truck around and raced downtown. They found a policeman directing traffic.

"We think we know this guy's name," Peppe said to the cop. "No matter what he says, he is not armed. Don't kill him."[21]

After dialing the wrong number for two hours, the Leon County police finally established communication with Marshall Ledbetter in the Sergeant at Arms suite a little after 10:00 a.m.[22] The SWAT officers kept their fingers on the trigger of their assault rifles. They were decked out in camouflage gear, bulletproof vests, riot shields, and high-powered assault rifles. Every now and then Campbell would get down on his hands and knees and look under the door, trying to get a glimpse at Marshall Ledbetter.

Although it certainly took them by surprise and was not without its costs, the incident did provide certain benefits for the law-enforcement community. Not only did it provide a kind of dress rehearsal for an even more significant emergency, but it also allowed the police to experiment with their latest crime-prevention technology. Capitol Police had recently purchased a machine called the Hornet—an Israeli-built bomb-detecting robot with a camera—-which they hoped to use in situations like this.

The robust two-hundred-pound tank, built by a company called 21st Century Sivan, was about four feet long and three feet high.[23] It was equipped with video- and audio-recording technology as well as a swiveling 12-gauge, semi-automatic shotgun. According to South Carolina–based bomb technician and expert Jeff Fuller, the Hornet was designed to be "used as an observation platform on many SWAT responses," especially hostage situations, and "could be used to negotiate via audio/video with the perpetrator, deliver food etc. to a situation, illuminate the area, deliver breaching tools to doors and windows, and generally carry out tasks without placing an officer in harm's way."[24]

Jesse Lovett says that the Capitol Police brought out the Hornet because they were "concerned that he [Ledbetter] had the office booby-trapped."[25] This seems fair enough, but it is not clear how the robot would have made it past Ledbetter's barricade and into the Sergeant at Arms suite without Marshall's being alerted to its presence, not to mention how he would have reacted to it once it was inside with him.

Capitol Police wheeled the Hornet through the capitol on a hand truck and unloaded it outside room 403. But when they tried to deploy the machine on its inaugural mission, they found it to be non-operational. "Signal 7," Campbell says. "Didn't work." He says, "The robot would not start. It never left my side. I stood there, drank coffee, smoked cigarettes, and looked at it for a long time."[26]

At approximately 10:30 a.m., Campbell held another press conference, this time in the rotunda on the second floor of the capitol. He gave the now quite sizable press pool an update on the situation. Campbell said that Ledbetter had told them he would give himself up, but only if his list of demands was read live on CNN. "We're trying to save this man's life, right this minute," Campbell told the reporters." "The subject is talking with us. He has said that if a reporter . . . Mike Vasilinda . . . reads a list of demands, after he does that, he says he is going to come out . . . We're gonna do it on the in-house channel."[27]

A reporter asked, "Does he think this is going out live over CNN?" Campbell nodded.

"He does?" she repeated. Campbell nodded again.[28]

While some journalists might have been reluctant to stage a broadcast and cooperate with law enforcement in such a fluid event, Mike Vasilinda sensed the gravity of the situation and volunteered without hesitation.

Vasilinda had plenty of experience being live and on the air, and had in fact filed many stories with CNN over the years. Playing such a role now wouldn't require much preparation. Campbell gave him a copy of Marshall's demands note, and Vasilinda made a quick run-through. In the rotunda, he practiced reading Ledbetter's note in front of about twenty news people. Vasilinda had difficulty deciphering the meaning behind some of Ledbetter's demands, and also mispronounced "Flavor Flav." He was quickly corrected.

Having finished the run-through, Vasilinda was ready for the show. He was given the signal to begin. "I'm Mike Vasilinda reporting live from the second floor of the capitol, where two floors above us Marshall Ledbetter has taken over the Senate Sergeant at Arms office. Marshall, if you are watching this broadcast . . . the Sheriff's Department, the Leon County Sheriff's Department, has told us you that you will be safe, they assure us you will be safe, if you give yourself up. They have also given me this list of demands that they say you would like us to read."[29] Vasilinda then read Ledbetter's demands more or less verbatim.

At various times during the short broadcast, Vasilinda added a few editorial comments to his reporting. For instance, he said "Good choice" after mentioning Ledbetter's request for Asahi beer. He called Marshall's reference to the contents of the "liberated Iron Horse" a "puzzling request." And at the mention of the demand for a CNN news crew, he said, "We are here." Vasilinda closed the take by saying, "Marshall, again, I repeat: If you are watching this . . . the Leon County Sheriff's Office assures us that you will be safe if you give yourself up. I'm Mike Vasilinda reporting live from the second floor of the state capitol."[30]

Despite his cooperation with the police, the ethical aspects of a journalist suddenly becoming involved in a law-enforcement response to an ongoing criminal event were not lost on the broadcaster. "Immediately after the closed-circuit broadcast," Vasilinda says, "I was the subject of a gaggle asking the ethical questions. My general response was that if I could keep someone from being hurt or killed, then it was worth the effort. I would not have wanted someone dead because I refused to read a list."[31] Vasilinda adds that he "never intimated that I was live anywhere but on the inhouse system." He also says that he remembers Larry Campbell "suggesting that if I didn't [volunteer], Ledbetter, or one of his officers could get hurt."[32]

Vasilinda had done the best he could with the material he had. As Marshall had requested, his demands were indeed read "live on the air" by a CNN reporter. When the time was right, police negotiator Gilda Strickland simply told Ledbetter to tune in to the right channel in Wayne Todd's office and watch the coverage. But unbeknownst to Marshall, rather than going to CNN headquarters in Atlanta and then on to a worldwide audience, the closed-circuit broadcast never left the Florida State Capitol building.

Larry Campbell and the SWAT team continued to wait patiently outside the Sergeant at Arms suite. As Vasilinda wrapped up the broadcast, Campbell had his ear to the door. There were a few tense moments when it seemed like Marshall might not live up to his end of the bargain. Seconds later, Campbell says, he heard Ledbetter mutter a few words to himself. Marshall then opened the door and "came prancing out."[33]

Aftermath

I want to be feared. I want to continue to fight the power structure that ruins the planet.

Marshall Ledbetter, in Dr. William Spence, "Court-Ordered Psychological Evaluation," July 2, 1991

In the public world one can be made a "celebrity" overnight by the newspapers and journals. That always remains the surest way to have one's intentions get misinterpreted and quickly and thoroughly forgotten.

Martin Heidegger, "Why Do I Stay in the Provinces?"

Weapons locked and loaded, the SWAT team wasted no time subduing Marshall Ledbetter as he emerged from the Sergeant at Arms suite. "He was well covered," said Campbell when asked about the firepower pointed in Ledbetter's direction.[1] According to Campbell, the erstwhile FSU honors student had been having a "big time" that morning. He "had a fifth of Jack Daniels in one hand and a great big thing of cigars in the other hand and a big old cigar in his mouth—just having a really good time of it."[2]

While the SWAT team dealt with Ledbetter, Sergeant at Arms Wayne Todd was milling around nervously. He had just returned from Carrabelle and would have preferred to be back on the coast. He wasn't used to being the center of attention. Todd had started out as an aide to Sergeant at Arms Leroy Adkison back in 1968, when he was twenty-three, and had worked his way up through the ranks. Since 1982, when he took over the position from John Melton, Todd had been a significant behind-the-scenes player in Florida politics. He has been described as having a "bartender's ear for listening, a caddy's talent for giving discreet advice, a butler's ability to look the other way and the scrounging talent of an Army supply corporal."[3] His services as sergeant at arms ran the gamut from ordering supplies to arranging secret meetings between politicians and even setting up dates for the senators. "We called them 'road wives' back then," Todd told the Associated Press at his retirement party in 1999. "They were women the members were here with sometimes."[4] Todd would be involved with other kinds of hijinks, including what was known around the capitol as "'vodka Fridays' when the Senate's orange juice cooler was always spiked" and "former Senators Tom McPherson of Fort Lauderdale and Frank Mann of Fort Myers ran an open bar" known as "the M&M Room."[5]

Yet on this particular day, with all the law enforcement and media swarming around his office, Todd was worried about the negative publicity. He saw the Leon County undersheriff with the remnants of the alcohol Marshall had consumed during his occupation. Todd recalls: "I told Larry Campbell to get that liquor bottle out of his hand before the press got in to see us."[6] Of Todd, Campbell would remark, "I saved that old bastard's job."[7]

There are varying estimates of the condition of Todd's office after Marshall's eight-hour occupation. Senate President Gwen Margolis's press secretary, Gayle Andrews, said that Ledbetter had really torn the place up. Todd recalls that the suite was a little messy but "wasn't trashed or anything."[8] His assistant, Julie Anderson, remembers cigar ash, trampled African violets, and "stuff all over the floor."[9] One of the wooden doors to the suite had a chip in it from the smashed whisky bottle and would eventually be replaced.

The first images we have of Ledbetter that morning depict a barefooted, bespectacled, skinny young man in boxer shorts with an Austin Powers sort of hair patch on his chest. His arms held behind his back in handcuffs, he is being hurried away by a couple of serious-looking policemen. A few moments later, wearing his acid-washed shorts and Jimi Hendrix T-shirt, Ledbetter was escorted to the first floor of the capitol complex and out through the loading zone to a waiting patrol car. James McPherson, head of Capitol Police, led the way, clearing a path through the crowd of about thirty reporters, photographers, and television people. They lobbed questions to the wiry young radical. Ledbetter dealt with their inquiries diplomatically. Jackie Hallifax, an AP reporter, observed that Marshall "seemed composed" as he left the building.[10]

"Marshall, why'd you do it?" yelled one reporter. Ledbetter responded calmly and with sincerity: "I needed a soapbox." Someone else asked: "Is this how you fight the power?" Perhaps taken aback by this sudden reference to Public Enemy, one of his favorite rap groups— Marshall started to say, "Basically, when you're frustrated—" but was cut off by the further clamor of the corps.[11] In response to a subsequent barrage of questions, Marshall said: "I can explain this all, you know. But I can't describe it all in one sound bite. You'll find out." As he was finally being ushered out the door, his last words to the media were: "If I could synopsis it in three seconds, I wouldn't need a press conference."[12] Apparently, as part of the negotiations with Sergeant Gilda Strickland, Marshall had been told he would have a formal opportunity to address the media later that day. In retrospect, that was a promise he should have probably gotten in writing.

At about 12:45 p.m., almost ten hours since he arrived, Marshall left the premises of the Florida state capitol and was taken to the Leon County sheriff's office on Thomasville Highway. Tallahassee breathed a collective sigh of relief. People got back to their lives. Undersheriff Campbell held his final press conference of the day in the courtyard. Visibly relieved that the incident was over, he gave reporters a play-by-play account of Strickland's negotiations with Ledbetter. Campbell told the press how they had lured Marshall out by broadcasting Mike Vasilinda's reading of Ledbetter's demands through the building's closed-circuit television. Campbell said, "We did that part of it, everything went real good. And then there was a period of time [when] he wasn't coming out and that concerned us for a while. He subsequently came on out."[13]

The press corps inquired into Ledbetter's motives. Campbell responded as he had done earlier. "His demands are basically incoherent," he said. "The biggest thing he wanted [was] to talk to Timothy Leary." Then Campbell declared seriously (and, as it turned out, erroneously),

"Timothy Leary has been dead for some time as I am sure you are all aware."[14]

Whether no member of the press either knew better or dared to correct him, Timothy Leary was still very much alive. In fact, he would remain so for another five years. Two weeks after Ledbetter's break-in, the chain-smoking, seventy-year-old guru of 1960s counterculture would be paid $35,000 to give a lecture on virtual reality in Toronto, Canada.[15]

Campbell told the press that Marshall started crying when they told him about Leary's demise: "We broke the news to him after he was in custody and it broke him up." Campbell continued the briefing. He said Ledbetter "belongs to some group at FSU that he describes as the Monarch [sic] group or the Monarch Party."

A reporter asked the million-dollar question: "Why did he say he wanted to do this?"

Campbell chortled, "We don't have an intelligible answer on that at this point."[16]

A few moments later, on the steps of the capitol, Gilda Strickland, who had talked Marshall Ledbetter down and convinced him to surrender, offered her thoughts on the day's events. "He basically is a young man who is very concerned about what is going on in the world and the hunger and poverty that he sees and he wanted some way to say to the world that he wanted it to be better," she said.[17] A reporter asked her about Ledbetter's state of mind. "Most of the time he was very coherent," Strickland said. "He was of course very nervous when the conversation first started, but then he calmed down and we had a very pleasant conversation."

She added: "I think the young man has always wanted to meet a gentleman by the name of Timothy O'Leary [sic]. I don't know if y'all know Timothy O'Leary, but he had something to do with LSD way back when. And he wanted us to bring Timothy O'Leary here to meet with him so that he could talk to him about that."[18]

Someone asked: "What did you tell him?"

Strickland responded: "Well, I had to break the news to him first of all that Timothy O'Leary I believe is deceased at this time." She said Ledbetter was shaken by the news. "After that, some of the demands quieted," she said. Strickland also told the media that Marshall had been drinking that morning. Marshall had said to her, "I am a little bit drunk," as he was trying to turn on the television set to watch the broadcast.[19]

In describing the mechanics of the negotiation process, Strickland said that while speaking with Ledbetter "there was a rapport that was established. After a while I could tell that we were really talking with each other rather than at each other." Interestingly, she stated that in her view, Marshall was not despondent and there was no indication he was having any personal or family problems. She said Marshall made no threats at all and "there was no time" she ever thought the situation would become violent.[20] Strickland said the biggest issue Marshall was concerned about was poverty and that "he's very concerned about even the homeless people in Tallahassee." In her view, Ledbetter was "kind of your Robin Hood mentality . . . take money from the wealthy and give to the poor."[21] She referred to Marshall a "low-key individual" and said "poverty is his big thing."[22]

There have been only a few occasions in recent memory when Tallahassee would become the object of the world's attention. One was in 2000, when the outcome of the presidential election came down to a contentious recount and the city was the site of all the legal maneuverings in *Bush v. Gore* before the U.S. Supreme Court decided the case (5–4). For about a month back then—when it seemed like all the journalists in the world were in town—Tallahassee was the figurative center of the universe.

But the Ledbetter case shows that it certainly was not the first time the eyes of the world had been on Tallahassee. The flour-encrusted telephones at Gumby's Pizza rang off the hook with requests for the "Ledbetter Special," a twenty-inch vegetarian pizza with extra jalapenos.[23] One radio station declared it "Gumby's Weekend" and gave away free pizzas to callers.[24] *Tallahassee Democrat* writer Mark Hinson recalls it was a "sleepy summer night, a slow news day, and 'Boy, Howdy!'"[25]

Tallahassee was suddenly all over the news. Even CNN, the very network whose airwaves Marshall wanted to expropriate in order to broadcast his demands to the world, reported live updates throughout the day. Ledbetter's break-in was covered across the country and around the world. He was mentioned in Eugene, Oregon's *Register-Guard*.[26] In Australia, the story was picked up by Queensland's *Sunday Mail* and Sydney's *Sun Herald*.[27] Tallahassee business owner Gregory Cohen remembers getting phone calls about the incident from friends traveling abroad, one was in Ireland and the other in Moscow. Both callers said they had heard about Ledbetter through CNN International and wanted the scoop on what was going on.[28]

The local Tallahassee media were divided in their coverage of the case. Florida State's independent paper, the *Florida Flambeau*, was generally sympathetic to Ledbetter's plight and led the way in covering the story. The *Tallahassee Democrat* initially framed the break-in more as a safety issue and suggested that Ledbetter had intentionally subverted the building's complicated security system as he stormed his way into the building. The paper reported that Marshall had "found a weak spot in the Capitol's defenses, then exploited out-of-date security equipment to disappear into the maze-like interior of the building."[29]

In his afternoon press conference, Larry Campbell assured the media that the capitol was safe and secure. "A building that is as tall as this one is always a problem," he said. "They break into bank vaults, too, so . . . it happens."[30] Sooner or later something was bound to happen. He stated that the agencies charged with protecting the capitol had conducted a number of training exercises earlier that year to deal with cases like this. He expressed confidence that such training had been effective and said there were sufficient contingency plans in place to cope with any future threats to the building.

Lanora Mahler called Ledbetter's parents in Auburndale to tell them what had happened. They had already heard the news. Marshall's mother says that the event was "devastating for the family."[31] Ledbetter's parents were very concerned, upset, and frustrated about their son, whom they were trying so hard to help. Marshall Ledbetter Sr. would later tell his son's psychiatric examiner that he had seen a big change recently in his eldest son. Marshall had been acting strangely of late and "was definitely not as we knew him before."[32] Marshall's mother started to wonder whether Marshall might have "some kind of mental disorder."[33] The family was rightly worried that their bright honors student son, whom they loved deeply, was squandering his and their own resources, his education, and tremendous potential. Mike Vasilinda, who spoke with the family in his continued coverage of the case, sensed that "they'd had enough and were at their wits' end."[34]

The Ledbetter family was also trying to deal with the all the media who now were intruding on their lives. Television producers, reporters, and other media personnel descended on Auburndale. Marshall's mother says that it was a highly "traumatic couple of days." The media were "like piranhas, trying to pick flesh off the bone." The aggressive tactics of the media in covering the event made a horrible situation even worse. They rang the doorbells of their neighbors, "pushing microphones into people's faces."[35] The news crews then moved on to downtown Auburndale, where they started going into various small businesses asking them if they would like to talk about the town's most infamous son.

The atmosphere was decidedly more celebratory at Florida State University. News of the break-in and Ledbetter's arrest spread throughout the student community. "Free Marshall Ledbetter Now" was chalked in big block letters on sidewalks around campus, on Woodward Street, and at the entrance to the student union. Similarly styled T-shirts were printed on a shoestring budget and distributed across town. Someone found old FMLN (Farabundo Martí National Liberation Front) buttons in the university's Center for Participatory Education office and started handing them out to passersby who thought they had been made in support of Marshall Ledbetter, not to El Salvador's struggle for democracy in the late 1980s and early 1990s.

Student reporter Josh Mitchell filed the first of what would be a number of excellent news reports about the Ledbetter story for the *Florida Flambeau*. "Local residents and many people in the national media's earshot may still be trying to figure out Ledbetter's motives based on the 'disturbed college student' description bounded around by several sources covering the story," he wrote in the first article, "but a group of friends painted a profile of him that suggested a complex mind exploding with dissenting ideas and radical ambitions."[36]

One of those friends, John Griffin, conceded that Marshall had "obviously flipped out." Yet he tried to explain the motivations of his friend by saying that Marshall was "sick to death of what was going on in the world, felt helpless, and wanted to empower himself."[37] Griffin said Ledbetter "wanted to try to begin ending all the craziness in the country. He feels America's pretty screwed up right now."[38] "Everything he's done makes him look like a big cartoon character," Griffin said, "but he's really a human being who just cares a lot about what's going on around him."[39] Marshall's neighbor Jennifer Luther told the *Sarasota Herald-Tribune*, "Marshall is probably one of the more intelligent people I've ever met. He is very disenchanted with some of the social injustices in our country. And his way of acting that out is not always acceptable in a structured environment."[40]

At 1:30 on the afternoon of the break-in, Ledbetter gave an oral statement to the police at the Leon County sheriff's office. In the room with him were Sergeant John Livings, of the county sheriff's office, and Lieutenant Hansel Vause, Sergeant William Hartsfield, and officer Michael Edwards of the Capitol Police. Marshall had no attorney present. Ledbetter began by telling the officers he "was very upset and depressed . . . over school and world [*sic*] needs." When he was asked by the police why he had selected the Sergeant at Arms office as the exact location for his takeover, Ledbetter told them that the "office represented authority" and that he "hoped to find a weapon and arm myself for defense."

According to the statement, Marshall had "decided by this time that there would be a shoot-out and that he could picture himself in a blazing gun battle on camera. . . . Ledbetter seemed very disappointed at not having a weapon and again stated he could picture himself behind the desk with an M-1 rifle standing everyone off."[41] Since he could not find any weapons, Ledbetter said he "decided to use whiskey bottles to fight off [the] cops" instead. Marshall had "reconciled himself to the fact that he may die or kill someone attempting to remove him from the office." In response to a question about "how far he intended to go for the cause," Ledbetter told them, "kill or be killed, he didn't care."[42]

Asked why he had hurled a bottle at Ruby Dennis that morning, Marshall told the officers he thought she was a policeman. Ledbetter told the police he "would use the bottle as a tool on a male cop. As for a female cop he didn't think it would be very manly to hurt a female, although he would throw the bottle at her and then run like hell." The statement concluded with Ledbetter stating that he "knew he had fucked up and would have to face whatever. He also stated that the charges were immaterial and not significant at this time."[43]

Later that afternoon, Marshall underwent an intake interview for the Leon County Pre-Trial Release program. On the forms he filled out, Ledbetter listed himself as unemployed and answered "neither" in response to a question as to whether he rented or owned a home. To questions about dependents, cash, motor vehicles, debts, income, real estate, stocks/bonds, and the value of his home, he entered "zero." He claimed to be in good health and said he had never been treated for a physical or mental disorder or for drug or alcohol abuse.

Ledbetter entered the name "Raven" as an alias on the police paperwork. He listed two individuals as personal references: Steven Profit and Kate Catestekin. Profit, as we know, was a close friend at whose apartment Marshall was currently staying.[44] He identified his other reference as a student living in Deviny Hall, the building immediately west of Landis Hall on FSU campus. The spelling "Kate Catestekin" appears to be an inaccurate reference to Catharina (Cate) Stoecklin, a student with whom Ledbetter was becoming friendly at this time. Stoecklin, a mathematics major, ran in the same crowd as Marshall, namely, the one associated with the Monarchy Party and its offshoots.

The Monarchy Party was deeply concerned after hearing the news about the capitol. Key figures in the party organized a meeting to discuss their response. The Monarchists were used to creating spectacles, but they weren't sure what to make of this one. Marshall had mentioned the Monarchy Party by name in his demands note. Although Larry Campbell had mispronounced the name of their group, it was clear they were under some sort of investigation by law enforcement and were certainly being researched by the media.

They felt compelled to give their side of the story, so they decided to reach out to the press. A handful of Monarchists went to see editor Ron Matus at the *Flambeau* to provide some background information about Marshall and invite them to a press conference later that day. Matus remembers them showing up in the newsroom telling him, "That stuff you are hearing on the radio, that's Marshall Ledbetter. That is an FSU student."[45]

As it turned out, members of the *Flambeau* staff were already quite familiar with Marshall. In fact, they had received a number of incendiary letters to the editor along with various "Mushroom Cop" cartoons over the previous few weeks. Now they realized that the individual who had been contacting them was the same person who had just taken over the capitol.

The *Flambeau* would go to press the following Monday with the front-page headline "666 Jelly Doughnuts? Friends Insist Ledbetter Is No Loon." Reflecting upon the incident, Mitchell said that "there was no doubt the *Flambeau* would cover this story because we had, after all, been the news source he chose—and felt comfortable enough—to send his initial 'manifesto' and other issues to. Everyone at the *Flambeau* seemed to respect his ideals and so we went forward with the story."[46] Former *Flambeau* editor Ron Matus agrees. He says it was "definitely a story [that] was right for us. The sources were right there. We were super competitive with the other papers. We wanted to be all over it."[47]

At about 4:00 Friday afternoon, Andrew "Archduke" Arvesen—erstwhile King of the Monarchy Party—flanked by other members of the Royal Family, held a press conference in the pool area at the Campus Circle apartment complex on Basin Street in Tallahassee, just north of campus. Josh Mitchell remembers that there were "at least a dozen reporters there," including CNN. The cub reporter was now playing with the heavy hitters. "I remember at least two of those reporters had microphones or recording devices the *Flambeau* didn't have access to then," he recalls. "I had an old recorder but the CNN people were jamming their shit up in there before us college reporters had a chance to."[48]

Arvesen informed the press that the Monarchy Party was "very concerned about our friend Marshall" and "hoped he would be treated with respect by the authorities and get any help that he needed." Arvesen also "made it clear that the Monarchy Party had no part in planning nor any prior knowledge of his takeover." The Monarchy Party "hoped he was OK, and that everything would work out soon."

Looking back, Arvesen says he considered Marshall's situation primarily a "medical issue, a legal issue." He didn't think there was anything he could do, either individually or with the Monarchy Party, that could have helped. "I just didn't know what to do," he comments. "You know he had to know he was bringing a ton of bricks down on his head."[49]

Coincidentally, a fund-raising event for the Monarchy Party had been scheduled for the evening of Friday, June 14. Given the day's events, there was some debate about whether the party should proceed. Eventually, a consensus developed to go ahead with it. "It was a keg party at the swimming pool of the Plaza Apartments complex," Arvesen remembers. "It was a low-key affair. Just some beer and people hanging out, paying a few bucks cover charge to fund the Monarchists—basically like the old-time rent party idea."[50]

It turned out to be a strange night. Some attendees were excited about the capitol takeover and keen to celebrate Marshall's achievements with plenty of alcohol and good cheer. Others were shocked and curious to hear all the details. Lanora Mahler perceived a darker aura to the event, though, when she observed a couple of journalists staking out the party. It became clear that Marshall's behavior was no longer a local curiosity. She then realized that "none of us had any idea how big it all was."[51]

Marshall appeared in court the following day, a Saturday. Jasper Boehmke and Lanora Mahler witnessed the arraignment from the gallery. According to Mahler, Marshall looked "crazy and sad" during the proceedings.[52] Mike Vasilinda sent out a televised update of the case over the news wires. It ran like this:

Vasilinda: Twenty-two-year-old Marshall Ledbetter appeared to be coherent and in good spirits as he told the judge he had no job and no money. A public defender was appointed; he even chuckled when he was told why there would be no bond.
Judge: [Addressing Marshall—who was wearing his prison blues and had just stepped out of the jail's holding pen]: Based on the factual situation here, I think you should be screened. The court orders a psychological evaluation on this gentleman.
Marshall [interjects]: I'm sort of curious as to what sort of time frame you can give me for how long it's going to take to be

screened. Because I mean, since I came here basically I've been held incommunicado in this thirty by thirty inch cell . . .

Judge: . . . It won't take long . . .

Marshall: You know, I wouldn't really mind it except for that fact that . . .

Judge: Sir . . .

Marshall: . . . I haven't been given anything to read or . . .

Judge: Sir. . . . It won't take long.[53]

For his part, Ledbetter would have had little reason to worry about a psychological evaluation. He had no previous history of psychiatric problems, was a smart young man accustomed to standardized tests, and usually did quite well on them. But it was clear that Marshall Ledbetter was in trouble. He was facing a number of quite serious criminal charges: armed burglary, aggravated assault, and illegal broadcast over a police transmission. Obtaining a private attorney would be difficult given Marshall's precarious financial situation. Getting money from his family would have been unlikely if not impossible, especially coming on the heels of his DUI charge. No private attorney stepped forward to defend him, so a public defender was appointed. Marshall Ledbetter would here begin a relationship with the Florida justice and mental-health system that would endure for the rest of his life.

Searching for an Explanation

> What is at stake in everyday contemporary violence is not a king's divine right but the sacred core of respectability that the assailant is defending and defining through his violence.
>
> **Jack Katz,** *Seductions of Crime*

> I thought I even had Moses beat with my ACID acronym from my List of Demands back during the '91 Capitol bit. Annihilate Conditioning Integrate Data. I thought that was pretty damn hot.
>
> **Marshall Ledbetter, "Advice for Aspiring Messiahs"**

How do we understand what was happening to Marshall Ledbetter at this moment in his life? There is no question that Marshall was a deviant character. *Deviant* is a term sociologists use to describe someone who violates the normative code of a given culture. In many ways, Ledbetter had quite literally "turned from the straight road." At times he even transgressed the ideological boundaries of the already fairly nonconformist student subculture in which he was embedded. His close FSU friend Bert Peppe has described Marshall's behavior as "freaky deaky,"[1] and even punk rocker Jello Biafra—a person who has more than anyone publicly championed Ledbetter's story—suspects that "Marshall was having a serious meltdown."[2]

Of course, Ledbetter was acting in a deviant way. But deviance does not necessarily indicate pathology. For sociologists of deviance, it is wrongheaded to simply dismiss deviant social behavior as "crazy," "abnormal," or "evil." On the contrary, sociology tells us that this is where the really challenging thinking about the causes of deviance and crime should begin. As sociologist Jack Katz writes: "The challenge for explanation is to specify the steps of the dialectic process through which a person empowers the world to seduce him to criminality. On the one hand, we must explain how the individual himself *conjures up the spirit*. On the other hand, we must accept the attraction or compulsion as *authentic*."[3]

What happens to our understanding of the capitol break-in if we set aside for a moment the assumptions of the medical model of deviance and reflect upon Ledbetter's activity without the diagnosis of mental illness that would soon be affixed to him? Just how should one understand how Marshall got into his strange predicament? As he was being led away in handcuffs, Marshall seemed convinced he could rationalize his behavior. "I can explain everything," he declared. Ledbetter was apparently told he would be able to do so at a press conference that never materialized. Although he failed to realize it at the time, his "perp walk" *was* the press conference.[4] But what if Marshall had been allowed to have a press conference later that day? How might he have explained the situation? What would he have had to say to us about the motivations behind his actions?

Sociology provides a unique way to comprehend Ledbetter's break-in at the capitol, in that it illuminates not only what Robert K. Merton called the manifest (or stated) causes of the incident but the latent (or non-obvious) causes as well. In particular, I suggest we can learn a lot about Ledbetter's case by turning to Katz's innovative book *Seductions of Crime*, which offers an interesting framework to understand criminal behavior. Katz writes that most research on crime focuses on the wrong things. In his words, "The study of crime has been preoccupied with a search for background forces, usually defects in the offenders' psychological backgrounds or social environments, to the neglect of the positive, often wonderful attractions within the lived experience of criminality." In Katz's view, those interested in truly understanding crime and deviance should bracket such "background" forces and study "foreground" factors instead. Foreground factors are what Katz calls the "attractions" that seduce people into committing deviance. Katz's symbolic interactionist approach offers a useful way to interpret

Ledbetter's intervention at the capitol, which can be now conceptualized as an extraordinary, if bizarre, social accomplishment. "It is no simple matter to raise these spirits," says Katz.[5]

Following Katz's lead, the sociological focus is on how Marshall was seduced into storming the capitol building that June morning. In fact, this is not very difficult to explain. The building is less than a mile's walk from the Florida State University campus. Its shadow looms large over the city. If you live in Tallahassee, it is impossible to avoid the state capitol and the social relations that emanate from within and around it. Whether it is the building encroaching into one's field of view while driving around town, having to avoid all the lobbyists in the better restaurants during legislative sessions, or simply knowing that the "sausage-making" process is always at some level happening just a stone's throw away behind the scenes, the capitol is always there. In thinking of Tallahassee without the capitol building, one conjures little more than a sleepy backwater in the North Florida countryside, a rest stop between Jacksonville and New Orleans.

A capitol building is a highly attractive target for any protest, since it is the real and symbolic foundation of power in the state. Hegel claimed that the state is, or should be, the embodiment of the ethical community. If people believe that the government is not living up to their expectations, they often go to state and national capitols to voice their grievances and complaints. Similarly, Ledbetter might argue that he stormed the capitol to take issue with an institution that was failing to fulfill its constitutional and moral mandate to represent all of Florida's citizens. By breaking into or besmirching the capitol, Ledbetter would generate an enormous amount of media attention and reach a large audience. In the words of hostage negotiator Gilda Strickland, Marshall chose the capitol because this was "where he could make the best statement."[6]

Certainly, some of Ledbetter's statements contain troubling violent imagery. Marshall made references to hostages and weapons, and he issued a warning about possible harm coming to police officers. In spite of this, one can perceive in his rhetoric a parallel to the "righteous anger" expressed against the state by various subaltern movements throughout history. As Lemmy Kilmister, lead singer and bassist for the band Motörhead, puts it in his autobiography, "School kids get up to all kinds of shit, and after all, why not? That's their job, isn't it—to piss off their elders and give them a cross to bear; otherwise, what use are they?"[7]

Ledbetter felt a kinship with Lemmy, as well as with Jello Biafra, both of whom made careers for themselves stirring up trouble. Ledbetter likely looked up to them as a teenager might to a couple of delinquent older brothers. Biafra once bragged of roughing up an audience before a Dead Kennedys show. "You had people just sitting down waiting to have a good time," he said, "and we were not going to allow that. We went out and knocked all these tables over and showered them with beer and shampooed them with cigarettes."[8] Although many readers might not be impressed by such behavior, hardcore punk rock fans like Ledbetter might get a kick out it. Marshall considered himself an anarchist for whom most forms of order are suspect. Throughout his life he loved putting the screws to the system. People like Jello Biafra are so interested in the Ledbetter story because it seems to offer a great example of a sort of political practice known as "culture jamming."[9]

For readers unfamiliar with the term, *culture jamming* might be described as a quintessentially postmodern form of social resistance. It involves using existing cultural structures and practices against the existing consumerist, bureaucratic order. It has its roots in surrealism, the New Left, and situationism. An excellent example of culture jamming is the monthly Critical Mass bicycle rides in San Francisco, where on the last Friday of each month thousands of cyclists take over Market Street for the afternoon commute, effectively bringing automobile traffic to a standstill. Other projects involve "buy nothing" days, people painting bicycle paths on roads without them, or defacing billboards with messages critical of consumerism. The Occupy Wall Street movement in New York City in September 2011, which then spread across the country and the world, might be considered an example of culture jamming on a larger scale.

Did Ledbetter intend his capitol break-in to be some sort of culture-jamming project? Remember that Ledbetter had just four days earlier had a conversation with Florida's governor, Lawton Chiles, that aired on public radio over all North Florida. Chiles had told the young man that if Marshall really thought he had a good idea for the state of Florida, well, he should come by sometime and tell him about it. In Ledbetter's skewed worldview, such a statement would have been as good as an engraved invitation.

The peculiar nature of the capitol's architecture may have also played a role in Ledbetter's decision to occupy the capitol. As anyone who has driven into Tallahassee on Apalachee Parkway can attest, the State Capitol Building is not only hugely phallic in design but grossly testicular as well. While I understand that many readers might think that the analyses of Sigmund Freud are today no longer relevant, one wonders what the old boy might make of the Ledbetter incident if he could take a look at the structure at the very scene of the crime.

We must also attend to the important role of Native American culture in Ledbetter's worldview. Shortly before the break-in, Marshall apparently discovered he was part Native American. He started to think of himself as a "sacred clown" or "clown dancer." As anthropologist Barbara Tedlock writes, "Sacred clowns, although often portrayed as merely providing comic relief in otherwise deadly serious ceremonies, are in reality close to the heart of American Indian religion." As an example, she mentions the "Sioux clown, or *heyoka* . . . a man or woman who has received the greatest possible vision, that of the Thunder Being."[10]

Could Marshall have had a similar sort of sacred vision? He did, after all, announce his attack on the capitol in the name of "Smoking Raven in the Eye of the Great Storm." Clown dancing would have appealed to Ledbetter. He was used to and enjoyed making people laugh. As Tedlock puts it, in clown-dancing ceremonies "onlookers are opened to immediate experience by laughter or shock; their minds are cleared of whatever worries they brought with them."[11] There are other interesting parallels. Tedlock says all a clown has "is himself and his actions. In a word, clowns are poor, or at least appear to be. All over North America they wear shabby clothing or even rags; they beg for and even steal food. Poor though they may be, they are also powerful and potentially terrifying."[12]

Such considerations raise a highly interesting question. Was the capitol takeover just a big clown dance for Marshall Ledbetter? When we take into account his anarchist leanings as well has his fascination with the Church of the SubGenius (whose motto is, remember, "Fuck 'em if they can't take a joke"), such an interpretation becomes rather plausible.

Ledbetter's prankster proclivities would have been bolstered by the hilarity that often accompanies the psilocybin mushroom experience itself. "Laughing. Laughing. Laugh. Couldn't stop laughing," is the way Dr. Timothy Leary described his own first experience with mushrooms. Leary laughed at "his own everyday pomposity, the narrow arrogance of scholars, the impudence of the rational, the smug naiveté of words in contrast to the raw rich ever-changing panoramas that flooded my brain."[13]

It is worth pointing out that if you read Ledbetter's list of demands to people who are unfamiliar with the case, before long they burst into laughter. Even veteran broadcaster Mike Vasilinda couldn't keep a straight face when he was reading Marshall's requests verbatim on camera, when Ledbetter's life was arguably in the balance. Could it be that Ledbetter broke into and occupied the capitol to make a stand for the rights of the poor and the dispossessed, but did so in the form of a huge practical joke he hoped would get the world's attention? Journalists and writers would reprint his unruly prose about donuts, pizza, and beer and then go to great lengths to investigate all the obscure cultural references Ledbetter had mentioned in his note. Word would spread quickly, and before long news of Marshall's political protest would be virally transmitted all around the world. Given his statements about world revolution, it is clear that Ledbetter was hoping his intervention in Tallahassee would stimulate activists, anarchists, and culture jammers on a global scale and wanted people in other places to somehow join in or follow suit. If all went according to plan, eventually the whole planet would be in on the joke. Everyone would be laughing, Ledbetter most of all.

"It was hilarious. It's still hilarious. I was just telling someone that story yesterday," says Ledbetter acquaintance Gregory Cohen.[14] It is important to point out that early on in the coverage of the event, Marshall was not framed as being mentally ill. As Josh Mitchell wrote in his first article on the subject, "The capitol break-in, it seems, was just the culmination of months of high thinking and debauchery."[15] Reporter Allen Judd referred to Marshall as a "neo-hippie who wants to use rap music to express his concern about world affairs."[16]

It bears observing that more than a few people did get the joke. The *Orlando Sentinel* ran with the headline "Intruder Disrupts Capitol Funniest Home Videos Fodder in Odd Standoff." The *Sarasota Herald-Tribune* went to press with "8 Hour Siege Wins Cigar but No Pizza" on the front page. They continued the humor inside: "But Would Another Hour Have Gotten Donuts?" As Mark Hinson has noted, Marshall's storming of the capitol was certainly "more dada than deadly."[17]

There are intriguing family resemblances between Ledbetter's protest at the Florida capitol and the direct-action tactics of the anarchist Yippies such as Abbie Hoffman in the 1960s. Think of the Columbia University students who occupied administrative buildings as waves of student protest swept the campus in the spring of 1968. Take a look at the iconic photograph of activist David Shapiro sitting in President Grayson Kirk's office smoking a cigar. Although many activists from the 1960s are now enjoying retirement in the same bourgeois luxury they once decried as unjust, one still would imagine that they could, at some level, identify with what Ledbetter was doing. And this is to say nothing about the latest generation of protestors cutting their teeth on Occupy Wall Street styles of politics.

The political world in which Ledbetter found himself was as familiar to the 1960s activists as it is to us today. As Hunter S. Thompson has pointed out, in the United States by the end of the 1960s the entire question of meaningful political action changed considerably. "Somewhere in the nightmare of failure that gripped America between 1965 and 1970," he writes, "the old Berkeley-born notion of beating The System by fighting it gave way to a sort of numb conviction that it made more sense in the long run to Flee, or even to simply hide, than to fight the bastards on anything even vaguely resembling their own terms."[18]

Sociologically, Ledbetter's action might be used as a particularly useful means of illustrating Robert K. Merton's theory of deviance.[19] Merton suggested that deviance and conformity can be explained in terms of a trade-off between cultural goals and the institutionally available

Marshall Ledbetter exiting the capitol. Hostage negotiator Gilda Strickland is to his left. Photo by Donn Dughi, State Archives of Florida, *Florida Memory,* http://floridamemory.com/items/show/103458.

means to achieve them. In other words, people who cannot meet their goals through socially appropriate channels often turn to, or invent, alternative or deviant means of goal attainment instead. In many respects, Merton's theory seems to explain much of what was happening with Marshall. Consider his state of mind at the time. He had just turned twenty-two. He was broke and had been homeless since the end of the spring term. The smart overachiever, always the student at the top of his class, was suddenly being left behind. Many of his friends and acquaintances from Florida State University had completed their degree programs, were starting graduate school, and getting on with their lives. Marshall, however, was academically, socially, and emotionally adrift. He had recently sabotaged himself by blowing off his classes and taking psychedelic mushrooms for three weeks instead.

Psychologists Sarah Riley and Graham Blackman report that paranoia, anxiety, and feeling overwhelmed are among the top negative characterizations of the psychedelic mushroom experience.[20] These conditions would likely have magnified any existential angst (or in

Merton's sociological equivalent, *anomie*) that Ledbetter was experiencing at the time. In the weeks leading up to the break-in, Marshall was increasingly viewed as a pariah among his friends. By planning and executing his capitol "prank," it seems likely that Marshall was trying to regain some of the status he had recently lost among his friends and associates.

Sex—or lack thereof—was likely another source of frustration. As Bert Peppe quipped to his friend *Flambeau* editor Ron Matus just after the incident, "Nothing like psychosexual frustration to make a man want to save the world!"[21] All these years later, Peppe still considered this a reasonable explanation for what had occurred that day back in the summer of 1991. "If Marshall had been fucking somebody," Peppe says, "he wouldn't have taken over the capitol." He says the only real difference between himself and Marshall at the time (despite having money to buy himself dinner) was that "I had a girlfriend."[22]

Marshall's adoration of Paula Abdul and his fondness for raunchy—what Peppe says Ledbetter called "arthroscopic"—pornography indicates a robust, perhaps even festering, sexuality.[23] It might be that Ledbetter was trying to impress a new love interest, a certain Cate Stoecklin. Marshall's listing of her name on his arrest intake form indicates an attraction that might not have been reciprocated. But what better way to get a girl's attention than for the cops to go and talk to her while you're in the slammer?

At the heart of Ledbetter's break-in, of course, was his demands note. While the police were at first flummoxed in their attempts at interpreting it, a closer look reveals the document to be in fact a quite intelligible, caustic, and at times even witty piece of writing. Ledbetter's rhetoric invokes obscure cultural signifiers, to be sure, but they did not exist solely in his fractured consciousness. They referred to people and places in the real world, some of whom were honored to be so named.

Deciphering Marshall Ledbetter's demands note, which we presented in chapter 8 (see page 53), is a good exercise in hermeneutics. Let's see what we can make of this curious text.

Marshall titled this note "Black Wampum + Red Sticks." What does this mean? Wampum are beads made from clam shells commonly worn or traded by Native Americans. The black wampum signifies "disease, distress, pain, or anger, particularly when used as a background color in belt patterns."[24]

The "Red Sticks" reference is rich and complicated. The name "Red Stick" dates to the Creek creation myth involving two primordial twin brothers, Red Stick and White Stick. The brothers had two different personalities that were associated with the colors. According to American Indian studies scholars Jean and Joyotpaul Chaudhuri, "red is the color of active life, while white is the color of reflective life. Those individuals who showed an extroverted activism were designated red sticks, whereas others with a more reflective quality were labeled white sticks." Over time, "Red sticks gravitated toward the tasks related to the security and defense of the community, while white sticks tended toward the performance of the more civil functions of the community."[25] Marshall's use of the term might indicate that he was in some way trying to secure and defend what he perceived as his own community. Although White Stick believed that "fighting wastes energy," Marshall's sympathies lay with Red Stick, who tells us to "First fight it out, then talk."[26]

"Red Sticks" would also have been a historical reference to the Red Stick Rebellion of 1813 at Fort Mims in present-day southeastern Alabama. The attack by the Red Stick Creeks came on the heels of some of the most highly organized Native American resistance to white westward expansion. In March 1811, the Shawnee chief Tecumseh had addressed five thousand Native Americans at a meeting of the tribes at Tuckabatchee. He said to them: "Let the white race perish. They seize your land; they corrupt your women, they trample on the ashes of your dead! Back whence they came, upon a trail of blood, they must be driven."[27] Some of Creeks did not go along with Tecumseh and opted for a path of assimilation, but the Red Sticks, "insisting on their land and culture," followed Tecumseh's lead.[28]

In July 1813, U.S. forces ambushed a group of Red Sticks as they were returning from Pensacola, loaded with provisions. In retaliation, the next month hundreds of Red Stick warriors stormed the garrison at Fort Mims and killed at least 250 people. The Alabama Historical Association calls it "most brutal massacre in American history."[29] U.S.

forces would get their revenge the following spring at the Battle at Horseshoe Bend. On March 27, 1814, Andrew Jackson and his men went to war against the Red Sticks, killing eight hundred, which ended the rebellion.

After the Red Sticks reference, Ledbetter discusses hostages. One of the reasons police became so concerned about the break-in at the capitol was the reference to a "hostage situation" in the second line of Ledbetter's demands note. Along with the mention of "hostiles" at the bottom of the page, the word "hostage" was taken by the police as a strong indication that this was no joking matter. It provided all the evidence needed for the high-powered response from the SWAT team. Yet one also notes that the whole sentence is clearly in quotes, in the third person, and spoken from the vantage point of an imaginary police officer. In making such a stylistic move, it seems Ledbetter was not writing representationally, but rather obliquely, akin to the sort of sample of police dispatches one finds in movies or in rap music.

Next, Marshall mentions Gumby's Pizza, the quintessential college pizza joint, which has numerous locations throughout the South. The chain is named after the iconic clay television character of the same name, who, along with his hapless horse, Pokey, entertained thousands of viewers in the 1950s and 1960s and then again on MTV in the 1980s. Gumby's specializes in large, cheap pizzas, pepperoni rolls, and the delectable Pokey Stix. Gumby's pizza was a staple in Marshall's diet, and it is rumored that he worked there. Gumby's occupied a special place in Ledbetter's world. Although Marshall tried to swindle many a business with his odd payment schemes and creative readings of credit card agreements, friend Chris Kittrell said that Marshall "never wrote a bad check to Gumby's."[30]

Moving on to Marshall's beverage request: Asahi Dry is high-end Japanese beer that you might find at your local sushi restaurant. I have never heard of anyone buying it by the case.

Lucky Strikes is a famous brand of American cigarettes, the choice smoke of President Lyndon Baines Johnson as well as Jean-Paul Belmondo in Godard's classic New Wave film *À bout de souffle* (1960). Ledbetter may have also mentioned this particular brand as a nod to the slogan "It's toasted," which appears on the back of the Lucky Strikes packet. In the vernacular of the 1990s, to be "toasted" means to be completely high on drugs or alcohol. Ledbetter's consumption in recent weeks of hundreds of psilocybin mushrooms, other drugs, and vast quantities of alcohol would certainly place him in such a category.

As noted earlier, the Iron Horse was the car that Marshall had "liberated" by not returning the vehicle to Budget Car Rental. The "contents" he refers to are the items taken by police during his arrest.

"Indica" is a high-potency, expensive marijuana.

CNN was one of Ledbetter's favorite television stations.

A police scanner would tell Ledbetter when the authorities were coming to get him.

Ledbetter's demand for "666 Dunkin Donuts for my fine friends in the TPD, FSUPD, and LCSD" signifies two tropes in American culture. The number 666 is the biblical sign of the devil or the "beast," and it is also a metaphor for law enforcement in gangsta rap. In bringing up the subject of donuts, Marshall is referencing the assumed propensity for police officers to eat donuts while on the job (think, for example, of Chief Clancy Wiggum from the animated television show *The Simpsons*).

Chinese food from the Asian Wok was fresh in Ledbetter's mind given the feast (discussed earlier) he and his friends had just enjoyed at the restaurant on Ledbetter's dime.

Requiring that these items "be delivered by anyone in the upper echelon of the Monarchy Party" was a reference to the FSU student group mentioned above. In mentioning the Monarchy Party in the context of his capitol break-in and occupation, Marshall likely thought he was practicing a kind of comedic one-upmanship on his comrades. The Monarchists had offered a severe, satirical critique of campus culture. Ledbetter would take such a spectacle to a wholly other level.

Ledbetter's note also demanded meetings with various individuals, more or less famous cultural and political luminaries of Ledbetter's day. Dr. Timothy Leary, named first and discussed earlier, was a psychology professor in Harvard University's Department of Social Relations from 1959 to 1963 before he was dismissed—ostensibly for not teaching his classes, but more likely due to his controversial experiments with mind-altering substances. Given his background and experiences, Leary would not only have been able to keenly understand Ledbetter's state of mind that morning at the capitol but might have shared his own experiences with law enforcement and institutionalization. Ledbetter appreciated Leary for his pioneering thoughts about virtual reality as much as his ideas about consciousness-expanding drugs. Friend John Griffin said Leary's ideas had inspired Ledbetter to "want to start a college based on Virtual Reality."[31]

Lemmy Kilmister is the lead singer of the English hard-rock group Motörhead. Although it sounds like the band is named for someone who likes to work on cars, a motorhead is actually a "speed freak," a user of amphetamines. Ledbetter named his rented Lincoln Town Car "Iron Horse" after the Motörhead song of that title. Kilmister's experimentations with LSD, his prodigious consumption of stimulants, and his reputation for staying up for days on end were also likely sources of inspiration for Marshall.[32] In the late 1960s it was reported that Kilmister and sound technician Dik Mik took amphetamines every day for "a few months" in order to experience "how long the human body can be made to jump about without stopping."[33] Although Kilmister—who will turn seventy in 2015—says he used to consume a bottle of Jack Daniels a day, he stated in 2012 that "now it's more like half a bottle."[34]

Jello Biafra (aka Eric Reed Boucher) is the former lead singer of Dead Kennedys, one of the more politically astute American punk rock bands. From the late 1970s to the early 1980s, Dead Kennedys recorded four albums: *California Über Alles*, *Fresh Fruit for Rotting Vegetables*, *Frankenchrist*, and *Bedtime for Democracy*. After the breakup of the band in 1986, the left-wing Biafra entered the countercultural lecture circuit by giving spoken-word performances. He also continued making music with other artists such as his old friend Al Jourgensen from Ministry. The *Los Angeles Times* has referred to Biafra as "one of rock's intelligent spokesman."[35] For decades, his "scathing and satirical" songwriting has struck "a chord with listeners disenchanted with the status quo."[36] Ledbetter's friend Chris Boose says that Marshall "idolized Jello Biafra, and Jello returned the favor in his own way."[37]

Ice Cube (aka O'Shea Jackson) is a well-known and successful rap artist who gained fame with the rap group N.W.A in 1988 with their popular but controversial song "Fuck the Police." The popularity of the song symbolized the dominance of gangsta rap in the culture industry. Although cultural conservatives in the United States condemned rap music for its violence and sexism, other listeners applauded its incipient critique of social and political institutions. One finds a lot of symbolic bravado and rhetorical threats against the state in rap music in general and in bands like N.W.A and Public Enemy in particular. Marshall Ledbetter would have been well acquainted with Ice Cube's powerful album *AmeriKKKa's Most Wanted*, released in the summer of 1990 to popular and critical acclaim. The work stood as Ice Cube's most political work until *The Predator* was released in the fall of 1992 in the wake of the Rodney King riots. Ice Cube managed to appeal to both black and white audiences. His songs gave rebellious white youth a way to identify with the trials and triumphs of the black underclass and gave listeners (of all races) the words and sounds to challenge their oppression.

Flavor Flav (aka William Drayton Jr.) was a founding member of the rap group Public Enemy, another of Ledbetter's favorite bands and arguably the most politically significant rap group of all time. The band was inducted into the Rock and Roll Hall of Fame in 2013. Like Ice Cube and Ice-T, Public Enemy was highly successful at crossing over to a white audience and even toured with white heavy-metal bands such as Anthrax and the gothic rock band Sisters of Mercy. It would not be at all surprising if Ledbetter had the opening lyrics to the Public Enemy song "Black Steel in the Hour of Chaos" in his head as he was breaking into the capitol: "I got a letter from the government the other day / I opened and read it, said they were suckers." Flavor Flav does most of his creative work as the group's "hype man," adding statements of emphasis (e.g., "You tell 'em, Chuck"; "Yeah, boy!") to complement Chuck D's rapping. Flav is easy to identify by the huge analog clock dangling from his neck, symbolizing that he knows what "time" it really is. Ledbetter would have appreciated Flav's wackiness and sense of humor.

The abbreviation AIM refers to the American Indian Movement, an organization that propelled the issues and interests of Native Americans to the national stage in the late 1960s and early 1970s. Although its legacy is by no means uncomplicated, for a short, intense period "AIM—and the promise of a movement that would organize and give

David Shapiro sits at the desk of Columbia University president Grayson Kirk during a sit-in on April 23, 1968. It is likely that Ledbetter imagined himself in an event of comparable historical significance. Like the student protestors at Columbia who helped themselves to President Kirk's madeira and fine cigars, Ledbetter would spend the morning of June 14, 1991, drinking Wayne Todd's bourbon and smoking his Hav-a-Tampa Jewels. Photo courtesy of Blake Fleetwood.

voice to a growing chorus of the voiceless in Indian communities—exploded across reservations and cities from North America to the Pacific Northwest."[38] As we have seen, Ledbetter claimed he was part Cherokee and considered himself a kind of "clown dancer." Ledbetter was deeply interested in Native American spirituality and culture. He would have likely known a good deal about the "Red Power" occupation of Alcatraz Island in the San Francisco Bay in 1968 and 1969.

Ledbetter's break-in at the capitol also has interesting similarities to AIM's takeover and occupation of the Bureau of Indian Affairs (BIA) building in Washington, D.C., during the 1972 presidential election. Renaming it the "Native American Embassy," AIM held the building for about a week in what activist Paul Smith and historian Robert Warrior describe as an act of "revolutionary hooliganism."[39] Protestors erected a giant tipi on the BIA lawn. Activists "barricaded doors with furniture and littered hallways with reports, memos and other paperwork from filing cabinets. War paint appeared on the faces of Indian men."[40] Like Ledbetter's occupation of the Florida capitol, the BIA event would be mainly recalled as a "fiasco" with its "comic and ironic moments."[41]

While by no means excluding the possibility of other interpretations, such an analysis should allow us to consider Ledbetter's note, "Black Wampum + Red Sticks," as a kind of agitprop art. The political and cultural figures mentioned in the note represent what criminologist Lonnie Athens calls "phantom companions," cognitive representations of significant others that exist in our minds and influence our thoughts and action.[42] Although he was alone when he broke in to the capitol, Ledbetter brought a host of phantom companions along with him. This is an essential point to keep in mind as we evaluate and try to understand deviance. As Richard Rhodes writes, "Violent actors act violently not because they are mentally ill or come from violent subcultures or are brain damaged or have low self-esteem but because they have different phantom communities from the rest of us."[43]

Incompetent to Proceed

So you're gonna be institutionalized
You'll come out brainwashed with bloodshot eyes
You won't have any say
They'll brainwash you until you see their way.

Suicidal Tendencies, "Institutionalized"

Even a blind pig of a shrink will stumble upon onto a truth truffle now and again.

Marshall Ledbetter, in Pudlow, "Resistance to Treatment Confounds Doctors, Courts"

Marshall Ledbetter was offered lithium by Dr. Ines Bragado-Spence soon after being admitted to the Leon County jail.[1] This drug, which, according to David Healy, is "neither an antidepressant, antipsychotic, nor tranquilizer," has been used since 1948 to treat bipolar disorder (or manic depression).[2] Psychiatrist Kay Jamison writes that "there can be no serious question" that lithium is "enormously effective in treating manic depression and preventing suicide."[3]

The chemical is not without its negative side effects. Lithium has been known to intensify depressive symptoms in some patients, and in concentrations just two or three times the therapeutic dose it can cause "potentially irreversible neurological damage, and coma or death."[4] Although newer drugs are now available to treat manic depression, lithium is still widely used today.[5]

Dr. Hugh Lunan, a professor of clinical pharmacy at Florida A&M University, told *Flambeau* reporter Josh Mitchell that lithium can have side effects ranging from "slurred speech and muscle spasms to confusion." He said: "It's a bad chemical but it's the only thing to give. . . . It's like treatment for cancer: you lose the hair and break the bone but live."[6] Jamison notes that adverse reactions to the drug include "occasional cognitive slowing and memory impairment" and that "some patients on lithium reported feeling that life was flatter and more colorless than it had been before."[7] Ledbetter knew all about the negative effects of lithium. He refused Dr. Bragado-Spence's medicine. "These psychotropic drugs are really powerful," he explained to the *Flambeau*.[8]

On June 19, Ledbetter's court-appointed attorney, Randolph Murrell, filed a motion to set bail. "The defendant is not a threat to himself or others [and] has no prior criminal convictions," he wrote.[9] Judge William Gary denied the request.

The next day, psychologist William E. Spence informed the court that he had completed a preliminary psychological examination. He said that Marshall was of "superior intelligence" but also that he was suffering from "bipolar disorder of the manic type." Spence pulled no punches in offering his recommendation: "Bottom line, he needs treatment."[10] The judge agreed and ruled that "Mr. Ledbetter does not have the capacity to participate in his defense at this time."[11] Gary ordered further psychological testing to be administered over the following weeks. In the meantime, Ledbetter would remain incarcerated.

There are conflicting accounts of Marshall's conditions of detention at the Leon County jail. In a letter to the editor, Marshall's friend and fellow FSU student Ridge Hardy told the *Flambeau* that Ledbetter was being kept in a three-by-three cell that required him to "sleep standing up." Hardy alleged: "They're not giving him his mail and they have him in a perpetual state of evaluation. They don't let him see sunlight for days on end."[12]

Such reports were contradicted by Marshall's attorney and by Larry Campbell. Murrell told the paper, "The jail has some authority to review mail or censor it, but I don't know any case where the jail didn't allow any mail."[13] Campbell flatly denied Hardy's claims and suggested that Ledbetter was "making up a bunch of things and trying for maximum publicity." He said Ledbetter was "making a lot of complaints that are just not happening. . . . Keeping his mail from him would be a federal offense." Campbell added: "He's sending *us* mail. . . . He's letting us know he's thinking about us."[14]

On June 21, Murrell filed with the court a "conditional plea of not guilty" in which he stated that the "defendant demands a trial by jury."[15]

Six days later, Ledbetter tried to escape from the Leon County jail. The details are fuzzy, but Bert Peppe recalls hearing that Marshall tried to suspend himself—spider-like—in the corner of his cell, and was planning on overpowering an unsuspecting guard coming through the doorway. Any such effort must have been quickly squashed, however, and given the absence of any further charges filed against Marshall, was probably dismissed as a joke. But after the escape attempt, Ledbetter told the press that jail staff kept moving him around the facility. He also complained that he had "only been up to the roof twice" for recreation and fresh air.[16]

Ledbetter says he was preyed upon by the Leon County jailhouse ministers, but refused their counsel. "They thought I'd have one of these religious conversions, but once a Christ-er realizes you're not one of those bulls—t types who's gonna believe, they avoid you," he said.[17] Always the avid reader, Ledbetter was nonetheless forced to spend much of his time reading the Bible due to lack of alternative reading matter. He would say to Josh Mitchell, "The Bible's a beautiful text but the Christians just don't know how to interpret it. The Bible is a combo text book on quantum physics relativity and sociobiology. When they say God created light and dark,that is the earliest recognition of neural networks. God is a neural network. . . . God is the human forebrain."[18]

Ledbetter reflected on his monotonous day-to-day routine at the jail: "In jail, your entire day is a succession of reminders that you're in county blues. The food sucks, and when it's time to eat they say 'feed up.'"[19] He also complained of having no television. Yet in spite of his deprivations, Marshall tried to play up his storming of the capitol for all it was worth, basking in the glow of his newfound fame. Ledbetter considered himself a prisoner of war. "Every day the public furor grows, and every day I get a little sharper, a little meaner, a little funnier, a little tighter," he announced in a letter to Larry Campbell.[20]

In fact, Ledbetter had indeed become a minor cause célèbre, and more than a few Tallahasseans were sympathetic to his plight. Craig S. Files, for example, wrote a letter to the *Flambeau* expressing his outrage over how Ledbetter's case was being handled. A U.S. Navy veteran and business student, Files asked rhetorically: "Since when is it a crime to be manic depressive?"[21]

In Files's opinion, Marshall was "anything but dangerous." He continued: "Well, he may be dangerous to the 'Redneck Piece of Mind' that seems to permeate this so-called city, but no danger to anyone's physical well-being. . . . The man is guilty of breaking a window and locking a door. All he did was say 'Look at me, Capitol security is so bad even I can break in.' . . . Marshall Ledbetter is a 'HERO.' He is simply an impatient youth acutely aware of the injustice of the world with no way to vent his frustration. He stands with those with no other way to be way to be heard."[22]

Yet Marshall also had his detractors. Tallahassee resident Ingemar Harris wrote that he objected to that idea that Marshall's break-in at the capitol had just been a prank. "I hope somebody can explain the humor," he said. "The entire law enforcement community was mobilized to deal with this situation. Ditto for the rest of the public employees whose job it is to protect our lives. They didn't know it was a 'prank.' They treated it like any other emergency situation and responded accordingly. What would have happened had a real emergency occurred at the same time?"[23] No doubt Harris's perspective was shared by many other Tallahassee residents.

Meanwhile, back in the jail, Marshall was about to undergo more investigations into his competency to stand trial. Randy Murrell, Ledbetter's attorney, says that Marshall underwent the testing voluntarily. There was "no suggestion that [Marshall] did not want to be examined," he says.[24] Murrell states that although the break-in had begun as a "prank of sorts," it soon "became clear that there were serious emotional and mental problems" below the surface.[25] Murrell recalls that Marshall was "fairly shy, but had a sense of humor." He says Marshall was "not a difficult client" and "was easy to work with."[26]

According to Florida Statute 916.12(1), "A defendant is incompetent to proceed . . . if the defendant does not have sufficient present ability to consult with her or his lawyer with a reasonable degree of rational understanding or if the defendant has no rational, as well as factual, understanding of the proceedings against her or him." In determining whether or not an individual is competent to proceed, 916.12(3) directs examiners to "report the defendant's capacity to: (a) Appreciate the charges or allegations against the defendant; (b) Appreciate the range and nature of possible penalties, if applicable, that may be imposed in the proceedings against the defendant; (c) Understand the adversarial nature of the legal process; (d) Disclose to counsel facts pertinent to the proceedings at issue; (e) Manifest appropriate courtroom behavior; (f) Testify relevantly; (g) Any other factor deemed relevant by the expert."

The question of mental competence is different from, though it can be related to, mental illness. According to Florida law, a person is "mentally ill" when he or she experiences the "impairment of the mental or emotional processes that exercise conscious control of one's actions or of the ability to perceive or understand reality." Statute 394.455(18) states that this definition of mental illness "does not include . . . intoxication, or conditions manifested only by antisocial behavior or substance abuse impairment."

On June 28, Marshall underwent a second round of psychological testing. Spence found Marshall "sitting on the floor, with his arms and legs crossed and his head lowered."[27] Marshall noticed the psychologist and said: "We have gone through this before, but here I am. I am a prisoner of war. What can I do? I am at your mercy and I'll do whatever you tell me."[28]

Spence wrote that Marshall was cognizant of his predicament and "oriented as to time, place, person and legal charges."[29] But he had serious doubts about Marshall's state of mind. In response to a question about his attorney, Ledbetter was quoted as saying, "I don't trust him. He's a lying pig. I gave him letters to deliver to CNN, and he returned them a week later and told me that it would not help my case, [so] that's what I'm dealing with."[30] Spence noted that Marshall wanted a new attorney.[31] Marshall said to him: "I would really like an ACLU lawyer, and if they want to they can bring in someone from the Sex Pistols, anyone who has a mindset to create a little action in that courtroom."[32]

In response to a question about his comprehension of the seriousness of the charges against him, Ledbetter said: "It's like a clown dance. No jury in the free world would convict me. I am going to say not guilty. Well, I might plead guilty to mischief, but not criminal mischief."[33] Clearly, Ledbetter was planning to use a potential courtroom appearance as a means to further his political ambitions and turn any trial into a mockery of the court system. Marshall told Spence that he wanted to "freak them out in court."[34] He went on: "If I were to go to court today—you remember the Chicago Seven and the gag rule on Bobby Seale. . . . It's all a puppet court. . . . I've got all this to the point where there is going to be a lot of hype, and I'm not going to be polite about it to the courts anymore."[35]

Ledbetter was referring, of course, to the infamous 1968 trial of Abbie Hoffman, Jerry Rubin, Tom Hayden, Bobbie Seale, and four other members of the so-called Chicago Eight, accused of masterminding the riots that took place outside the Democratic National Convention in Chicago. The hearing ranks among the most spectacular and politically charged court proceeding in the history of U.S. jurisprudence. Hoffman appeared in court in wearing judicial robes (with a Chicago Police Department T-shirt underneath), spoke to the judge in Yiddish, yelled obscenities, argued that Jesus was a Yippie, and made other highly unusual legal maneuvers. Black Panther Bobby Seale also ridiculed the court, for which he was charged with contempt and then ejected from the courtroom.[36]

Marshall didn't back down when Spence pressed him on his motivations for his crime. He said he was "totally right" for breaking into the capitol. Ledbetter declared, "I did what I had to do, to go out and fight for freedom to do what we must do. This was a declaration of war on the present day power structure of this planet. I was doing my best to invite a world revolution, all over the planet. . . . My bottom line is they are my enemy, all those in power who speak lies. I must get the world's attention and what I did was right."[37]

Spence wasn't convinced. He described Marshall as almost a textbook case of mania: Marshall was "in a state of euphoria" with "grandiose, expansive thoughts." He documented Marshall's "racing thoughts," "pressured speech," "flight of ideas," "inflated self-esteem," and "decreased need for sleep." Even more importantly, Spence declared that Marshall had actually been insane when he broke into the capitol. Spence said: "There are two questions to be answered relative to sanity at the time of the alleged offense: 1) Did Mr. Ledbetter know what he was doing? Yes. 2) Did he know what he was doing was wrong? No. He was insane at the time of the alleged offense in accordance with Florida law."[38]

Echoing his earlier finding, Spence diagnosed Marshall as suffering from "bipolar disorder of the manic type" as well as "psychoactive substance abuse." Due to his mental illness, Spence said, Ledbetter was incompetent to stand trial. He offered two remedies. One was for Marshall to stay in Leon County jail and take "prescribed medication . . . in order for him to attain competence." However, since Marshall had already stated that he would refuse such medication, the examiner said this was not a viable option. Spence said the only other possibility for Marshall was "a structured inpatient treatment program in a psychiatric hospital." He concluded his report: "There is a likelihood that [Marshall] will attain competence in the foreseeable future. The time frame . . . will depend on Mr. Ledbetter's cooperation and his willingness to take medication and to be stabilized relative to his mental illness. At this time, Mr. Ledbetter refuses to accept the fact that he has a mental disorder."[39]

On July 12, after being in custody for about a month, Marshall underwent a third psychological assessment, this time with psychologist J. Kenneth Kling. Upon meeting Marshall, Kling found him "euphoric with his mood reflecting optimism, self-assuredness, and friendliness. He was well oriented as to time, place, person and circumstance."[40] Kling noted that Ledbetter's "memory functions were appropriately intact." There was "no evidence to indicate that he was hearing imaginary voices or perceiving imaginary visual events or having other sensory experiences that would have no basis in fact. . . . Nothing was detected which would indicate that he had ever experienced psychiatric difficulties in the past. . . . His motoric behavior was considered to be within normal limits. . . . He is currently not considered to be a physical danger to himself or others."[41]

Regarding the question of competency, the psychologist wrote that Ledbetter "fully appreciated the charges against him . . . specified the difference between felonies and misdemeanors . . . had some understanding of criminal law procedures . . . [and] was able to easily identify the name and duties of most courtroom participants. . . . He was able to describe the initial argument process, cross examination, and final arguments. He also made mention that oftentimes juries are sequestered."[42]

Yet, in spite of this—apparently quite considerable—evidence indicating mental competency, Kling, like Spence, concluded that Ledbetter was "incompetent to proceed and insane at the time of the offense."[43] He based this opinion on a number of observations. Kling said Marshall was "suspicious, distrustful, easily threatened, and likely to over-respond to minor environmental stresses with belligerent behavior and emotional outbursts. He certainly demonstrates unrealistic and grandiose plans that have no basis in fact and generally would be considered bizarre by most people. Marshall views the world as a threatening place and he seems to feel that he is getting a raw deal out of life. He certainly endorsed a number of extreme and bizarre thoughts which indicates that he believes he has special mystical powers or possibly a special 'mission' in life which others do not understand or accept. He has an over-inflated view of himself and resents others making demands on him. He seems to have much past conflict with authority and is quite resentful of societal standards of conduct."[44]

Kling went on to suggest that Marshall did not have many positive friendships: "The available data indicate that Marshall experiences highly disruptive interpersonal relationships. His pervasive lack of trust and wariness of other people causes him to have problems relating to others. His lack of trust seems to prevent his development of warm, close relationships, in spite of his reports to the contrary."[45]

Dr. Kling didn't have a particularly sympathetic interpretation of the written messages that Ledbetter had left for police around the capitol. He wrote: "Analysis of the notes written to provide directions to law enforcement officers, as judged by Marshall's own explanations, also are rather bizarre and at counter purpose to his implied intention

to 'shame people' out of their 'apathy' into action that would culmi-
nate into a major movement against bureaucracy. . . . He was apparently motivated by idiosyncratic purposes produced by rather bizarre
mentation. It is apparent to the examiner that Marshall's actions were
not intended to be frivolous but were strictly a function of the 'virtual
reality' perspective which is obviously unique to Marshall."[46]

Kling concluded by concurring with the assessments of his col-
league. He claimed Marshall's behavior was congruent with the diagnosis of "Bipolar Affective Disorder, Manic Type with Mood Congruent
Psychotic Features."[47] Kling expressed worry that Marshall's condition
would prevent Murrell from doing his job. He wrote, "it is quite possible that [Marshall's] communication with his attorney will be inef-
fectual." Kling said Ledbetter's "behavior at trial is considered to be
unpredictable" and was troubled by Marshall's intention to testify on
his own behalf.[48] Kling quotes Marshall as saying, "Things might get
weird for Murrell. . . . I can testify more relevantly than anyone there;
I am going to screw with them. . . . I refuse to take lithium. . . . I plan
to plead innocent by reason of hyper sanity because I am above and
beyond the law."[49]

Kling reported that such outbursts "produced probably the most
potentially destructive and self-defeating aspect of Marshall's behavior" and that any testimony from Marshall "is apt to be tangential and
self-defeating." Marshall's ability to "aid and assist rationally" in his
defense was "tenuous," he said.[50] Kling continued: "It is apparent that
Marshall understands the legal process but really does not care, probably more of a function of some type of physical chemical imbalance
consistent with a major mental disorder rather than rational, calcu-
lated willfulness. Thus it seems likely that Marshall's attorney would
experience significant difficulty in planning a defense and managing
the case since it appears that Marshall and his attorney would be at
counter purposes following different agenda."[51]

In offering his recommendation, Kling wrote: "It appears to this examiner that the best course of action would be to have the defendant
hospitalized. While he is not highly aggressive, suicidal, or self-muti-
lative, he is non-compliant with treatment recommendations . . . and

certainly is not motivated to participate in any treatment program at this time. The examiner feels that appropriate psychotropic medication very well might cause him to become competent. . . . The examiner does not know of any facility other than Florida State Hospital at Chattahoochee . . . that could provide the needed control and supervision necessary to control Marshall's erratic, unpredictable and potentially dangerous impulsive behavioral tendencies."[52]

Upon submission of this third and final evaluation, the state of Florida's mental-health experts rested their case. They argued that Ledbetter was incompetent to face the charges against him. Such judgments would soon be accepted as the facts of the court and become the truth in the eyes of the law. At that moment, the course of Marshall Ledbetter's life changed dramatically. He was no longer a disaffected young radical with a peculiar ax to grind. As the power relations in Ledbetter's courtroom workgroup played themselves out, Ledbetter emerged from his assessments with a new identity—that of a psychiatric patient.

Marshall's examiners were unwilling to dismiss his actions as a prank, a protest, or even a willfully criminal act. Although Marshall performed adequately, and in some cases superbly, on a number of key measures of competency, he was also recalcitrant and unrepentant. Given the all-or-nothing nature of these competency examinations, Marshall was declared incompetent to proceed. Spence's and Kling's arguments boiled down to three essential concerns: Marshall would not be able to relate well to his attorney; he might engage in inappropriate behavior in the courtroom; and he would not be able to offer relevant testimony if placed on the stand.

According to Florida law, a formal competency hearing to consider claims of incompetence to proceed is not required before involuntary commitment to a psychiatric hospital occurs. Statute 916.12(2) states that if all parties agree, the court may, after receiving just one expert evaluation, conclude that "the defendant is incompetent to proceed and . . . may commit the defendant or take other action . . . without further evaluation or hearing."

In Ledbetter's case it appears that the judge was anticipating a competency hearing, but Murrell changed course once the results of the assessments came in. On July 22 he wrote to Ledbetter at the Leon County jail:

Dear Mr. Ledbetter,

Enclosed is a copy of Dr. Kling's report. Although I had thought he might reach a different conclusion, as you can see from the report, he has concluded that you were insane at the time of the offense and that you are incompetent to proceed.

You are currently scheduled for a competency hearing on July 31, 1991. However, given that both Dr. Kling and Dr. Spence concur, the State Attorney's office is willing to forgo the hearing and simply have the judge enter an order finding you incompetent to proceed and committing you to Florida State Hospital. I'm sure that would be the result if we wait until the 31st to have the hearing. Thus, rather than delay and keep you in jail any longer than is necessary, I am going to approach the judge and ask him to enter an order simply on the basis of the reports. That means there will not be a hearing.

It is conceivable you could still be at the jail for several weeks before you go to the hospital, but I am hopeful the hospital will move quickly. I'll be out to speak with you about the matter next week.[53]

We have no idea how Marshall reacted to this news, but we do know that he would have received the letter after his right to a hearing had been waived.

Although Murrell stated he would be "out to speak with" Marshall the following week, the next day, Judge Gary ordered that Ledbetter was incompetent to proceed and began the process of involuntary commitment. The order made only brief mention of the hearing. Pursuant to the court's earlier motion directing that "Mental Health Experts be Appointed for the Purpose of Determining the Defendant's Competency to Proceed," the court asserted that "the State and Defense stipulated that, in lieu of a hearing with the presentation of testimony that the Court could simply consider the testimony submitted."[54]

Perhaps nothing should be read into the fact that Marshall had no formal competency hearing as described in Florida *Rules of Criminal Procedure* 3.210b. Given the mention in the *Rules* about being "examined by no more than 3 experts," it seems Ledbetter had reached his limit. Of course, he had been examined twice by the same psychologist, and it would have been unusual for Spence to reverse himself. Even if another expert had declared Marshall competent to proceed, that viewpoint would have still been outnumbered two to one. Maybe Murrell just did the math and went with the majority opinion.

In commenting on the case, Assistant State Attorney Chris Canova told the *Flambeau* that the decision to declare Ledbetter incompetent to proceed was the correct one. He said Ledbetter would not relate well to his attorney and was a danger to society. Canova stated that Ledbetter's "ability to aid his lawyer in his defense is what the concern is." But then he added: "That's not to say that he's not dangerous. In my opinion, he is dangerous."[55]

Murrell did not raise any objections to the incompetency ruling. "The idea is, he goes to receive whatever treatment is necessary," he told the press.[56] Although it still might have been argued that Marshall was guilty of nothing more than being an inebriated slacker trying to pull off a bizarre prank at the state capitol, his psychological examiners thought otherwise. Florida State Hospital would sort him out.

Although the vast majority of people diagnosed with manic depression are never institutionalized, Ledbetter's biography does contain similarities to other individuals—in particular, creative, artistic people—said to suffer from this condition. Like them, Marshall exhibited "heightened imaginative powers, intensified emotional responses, and increased energy."[57] Dr. Nassir Ghaemi of Tufts Medical Center describes mania in the following way: "Mood is generally elated, even sometimes giddy, often alternating with anger. One doesn't need to sleep much. . . . One's thoughts pour forth; the brain seems to be much faster than the mouth. Trying to keep up with those rapid thoughts, one talks fast, interrupting others. Friends and coworkers become annoyed; they can't get a word in edgewise." Ghaemi argues that bipolar disorder sometimes "leads to great success. . . . But often it leads to equally grand failures."[58]

It is hard to read these words without seeing at least a glimpse of Marshall Ledbetter. Other evidence would seem to point in the same direction. For example, as a "gifted" child, Ledbetter would have had a greater propensity for bipolar disorder.[59] The peak periods for manic behavior are usually from April to September.[60] Marshall's vision quest and break-in at the capitol occurred in the spring; later in life, he would have trouble during the summer months. Manic depressives also exhibit "realism, resilience, empathy, and creativity"[61]—descriptors that all seem to fit Ledbetter's personality perfectly.

On the other hand, as Dr. Timothy Leary has noted: "A heavy psychedelic experience is upheaval time for anyone."[62] People also tend to do some very stupid things after drinking too much and not getting enough sleep. Perhaps another psychological examiner in a different part of the country or from a different cultural or professional background would have simply attributed Ledbetter's erratic behavior to all the drugs and alcohol he had been consuming. Maybe all Marshall needed was to get on the wagon, dry out, and clear the cobwebs from his mind.

Jamison writes that "two aspects of thinking in particular are pronounced" among people with bipolar disorder: "fluency, rapidity, and flexibility of thought on the one hand, and the ability to combine ideas or categories of thought in order to form new and original connections on the other."[63] Similar cognitive mechanisms are triggered by mind-altering substances. Was there a danger the psychological examiners were creating a false positive, that is, labeling Ledbetter mentally ill when in actuality it was mainly his substance abuse (along with his antisocial behavior) that was to blame? It does not seem that they stopped for a second to even consider the possibility.

On August 8, Judge Gary signed an order for the Leon County Sheriff's Department to transport Marshall to Florida State Hospital in Chattahoochee, forty-five miles west of Tallahassee. Ledbetter would spend the better part of the next four months there. If and when he regained competence, he would return to the Leon County Court to face charges of armed burglary of an occupied structure (first-degree felony), aggravated assault (third-degree felony), criminal mischief (third-degree felony), and unauthorized transmission on a police radio (first-degree misdemeanor). If convicted on all counts, he would be facing a maximum sentence of forty-one years behind bars.

Although Marshall might have been bitter about not getting a competency hearing, part of him must have been relieved to get to Chattahoochee. At least he was no longer inside the Leon County jail. Marshall had been there for almost two months already and was likely bored and fed up. Tallahassee family psychologist and former Chattahoochee psychology intern Tracey Morse thinks the Florida justice system was actually quite lenient with Ledbetter by sending him to Chattahoochee. "If they wanted to stick it to him, they would have let him rot in jail," she says.[64]

Although Marshall didn't have money and family resources to draw upon, he still had a substantial amount of social and cultural capital at his disposal. State officials must have known they were dealing with a bright, articulate, eccentric individual. Ledbetter was a white, middle-class, well-spoken young man. Given that he was a special case, so to speak, it seems he was handled (at least initially) quite carefully by the various agencies of social control with whom he interacted. It is likely, then, that Ledbetter's courtroom workgroup was driven as much by pity as by vengeance, perhaps more so. *Flambeau* writer Josh Mitchell thinks Marshall was "a lot better off in a mental hospital. I don't think he was treated that poorly by the state."[65]

Chattahoochee

If you're sane, and you don't want to be here,
why haven't you tried to escape?

From the film *Chattahoochee*

I wanted to be Ozymandias . . . until I went to
Chattahoochee.

Marshall Ledbetter, "Flossing"

Florida State Hospital, located in Chattahoochee, looks like something out of a William Faulkner story. Driving onto the six-hundred-acre campus, one enters a scene of whitewashed two-story buildings arranged in clusters on the sprawling grounds. Moss-draped oaks and rolling lawns envelop the spaces between the hospital's roads, sidewalks, and outbuildings. Only a few people are out and about. The aura is one of a ghost town, or a college campus during winter break.

The facility in Chattahoochee has an interesting history. Built in 1868, it was the state's first penitentiary. It might seem peculiar that the state didn't have an official prison before then, but remember that Florida was one of America's first, and also one of its last, frontiers.[1] Despite its sunny disposition, Florida has always had an edge about it. Florida's in-migrants include bankrupt debtors trying to salvage their finances, drifters and vagabonds, international celebrities and politicians, land barons and tourists, as well as the aged and infirm. Some of these folks eventually find themselves in Chattahoochee.

The prison was converted into Florida State Hospital in 1876 and had been operation for well over a century when Marshall Ledbetter was a patient in the early 1990s. Today, the institution—one of only three state-operated psychiatric hospitals left in Florida—provides services to about a thousand full-time residents who are either forensic patients (those associated with the commission of a crime) or civil clients, or who are in the dialectical behavioral therapy (DBT) program,[2] a form of therapy for "severely troubled people who don't respond to other treatments."[3]

Chattahoochee treats people across "a broad spectrum of personal characteristics, backgrounds, and mental health needs (70% men, 48% Caucasian, 44% African-American)."[4] The hospital lists "schizophrenia, bipolar disorder, [and] substance abuse" as common diagnoses of Axis I disorders, while "borderline, [and] antisocial" personality disorders are common Axis II diagnoses. A significant proportion of the hospital's residents come from "chronically underserved populations" and have "severe and persistent mental illnesses." Many residents have "dual mental health and substance disorder diagnoses, involvement with the criminal justice system, complicated medical conditions, cultural/ethnic heritages, and rural or inner city living circumstances."[5]

Visiting the grounds of the institution, you make your way past Chattahoochee's main administrative complex. You follow the road down toward Mosquito Creek, which flows into a medium-size lake at the back of the property. Here, the architecture takes a decidedly more modern turn. Southern gothic structures are replaced by stark, brick buildings and cordoned chain-link fences topped with razor wire. These are Units 23 and 24, also known as Forensics Services.

With 528 beds, Florida State Hospital's Forensics Services unit ranks "among the nation's largest secure inpatient forensic facilities."[6] Patients are between fifteen and eighty years of age and come from all counties in the state. In most cases, they have either been declared incompetent to stand trial or have been found not guilty by reason of insanity. Living conditions are considerably nicer at Chattahoochee than at a typical Florida county jail, let alone a state penitentiary. There are no locks on patients' doors, more privileges such as television and air-conditioning, and more frequent access to visitors.[7]

Upon admittance to Chattahoochee on August 8, Marshall underwent an "Initial Clinical Assessment."[8] Echoing the earlier diagnoses of Spence and Kling, Marshall was described as "rambling, tangential, and expressing a flight of ideas." His mood was reported to be euphoric.[9] He was checked in to Unit 23.

Before long, Marshall started getting visits from friends in Tallahassee. They would drive over in groups of four or five to see him. Jonathan Lammers recalls that "one of the first times we visited at Chattahoochee his eyes appeared to be watering constantly. . . . It really made me feel for him."[10] Overall, Marshall's FSU buddies were happy to see him coping in his new environment and say that he seemed in decent spirits given the circumstances. Jasper Boehmke remembers Marshall being much more "grounded" than he had been earlier in the summer.[11]

Yet we also know that Ledbetter resented and resisted his involuntary institutionalization. At the time of his admittance, it is likely Ledbetter found the idea that he was mentally ill not only laughable but also fascistic. Soon after he got there, Marshall "wrote letters to hospital administrators and to the [Tallahassee] Democrat expressing discontent."[12] In an interview with the Flambeau in early August 1991—in exchange for which he received two packs of Camel unfiltered cigarettes—Marshall aired his grievances.[13]

"They have to label me crazy because, otherwise, people might start losing their faith in the system," he said. "I just sort of feel like a bug under a glass to these people. I feel like a wolf in a pound waiting to be gassed—or in this case, injected."[14]

Ledbetter said he was spending much of his time "waiting for the court system to change its evaluation" and "unsuccessfully trying to make friends." Regarding his fellow psychiatric patients, Marshall remarked, "You try to communicate with these people and get nothing. But it's no worse than talking to a frat boy at Applebee's."[15] He described being at Chattahoochee as "surreal . . . weirder than any acid trip I've ever taken." Ledbetter mentioned "one black guy strapped down with four-point restraint [carrying on] this conversation with the ceiling."[16] "All we're doing here is wasting time," Ledbetter said. The authorities were "playing a ridiculous game. . . . They keep throwing me in the briar patch."[17]

Marshall said that transitioning from the Leon County jail to the state hospital was "sort of like going from hell to Purgatory. I've gone from a medieval dungeon to a state-of-the art dungeon."[18] At Chattahoochee he had his own room, decent food, and a library—he could even play an occasional game of pool. He also had access to television. But he complained of another patient, a "lord of the TV" who wouldn't let Marshall watch his favorite programs. "I'm going through withdrawal from data-net addiction," Ledbetter said.[19]

Marshall also told the *Flambeau* that what he really wanted was "a liter of Jack Daniels, a hit of acid and some copies of *Tiger Beat* magazine with pictures of Paula Abdul."[20] Marshall was still obsessed with Paula. He said he wanted her to write him and "be forever my girl. I'm M. C. Skat Kat come to life."[21]

When Marshall wasn't passing his time in such reverie, he attempted to draw even more attention to himself. A Secret Service agent paid him a visit after Ledbetter left an ambiguous voice-mail message for President George H. W. Bush at the FBI office in Tallahassee. Marshall had called "to tell Bush we both know what was contained in the Islamic Jihad message" and to "stop f—king around or we'll both end up dead."[22] Marshall also said he was threatening the U.S. government "with biological, chemical and nuclear terrorism until they start treating me like a human."[23] He appeared to think he could make such statements with impunity, since "the state's own label of insanity" had immunized him from prosecution.

"Wow!" Marshall said, "I am certified insane by the state. God, you don't know how much I am enjoying this. This for me is better than a diploma from FSU. I'm a psychotic biologist . . . an acid head physicist."[24] In a letter to State Attorney Willie Meggs he said that he was willing to "plead guilty to [the capitol break-in] if the state would drop all charges except for criminal mischief and the federal government would add to the list of charges treason, sedition and incitement of a riot—and then send me to the gas chamber."[25]

Despite the bravado, *Flambeau* reporter Josh Mitchell remembers that Marshall also seemed lonely and despondent at Chattahoochee. "It's not every day you see people of a genius-level intelligence in the state mental hospital," he says.[26] This assessment was shared by Ledbetter's friends Erica Sanz, Paul Wilbur, and Chris Boose, who made their own trip to the hospital later in the month. In a letter to the

Flambeau published on August 29, the group wrote that during their visit Marshall claimed that "he will be prohibited a trial by law until he submits to lithium treatment."[27] They said "Marshall sounded both rational and concerned about the effect of the drug on his ability to testify in his own defense."[28] Ledbetter's friends also said Marshall "has been provided with an overworked, underpaid public defender" and was "shackled by absurd rules that make it extremely difficult to contact other lawyers."[29] They went on to assert that "authorities have interrupted his mail, money, and personal items by failing to inform both him and his parents about 'insignificant' technical procedures."[30] They said they were setting up a legal defense fund for Marshall so that he could hire a new attorney.

About a week later, Judge Gary received a handwritten letter from Marshall Ledbetter. It read:

Your Honor,

I stormed the Capitol because it was my premise that, through individual action, it was still possible to, if not save, then at least help, not only oneself but also one's fellow man. I had already experienced, by their patronization of me and rejection of my beliefs, betrayal not only of my family but also the vast majority of those I believed to be my friends.

Now, by witnessing firsthand the refusal of those few I still considered my allies to undertake any significant, effective action to obtain my release, by seeing them still doing nothing but sitting around getting drunk, waiting impatiently for the massive, inefficient, state apparati to (maybe) spit me back out on the street after I have been sufficiently ground up at which time I will, obviously, somehow help them (because of course, no matter what he said or how empathically he stated it, it's obviously insane to even believe I could actually save my own soul), I have seen even them deny me.

Humanity says it hates to live in slavery, in fear, under the velvet covered iron glove of Sugar Daddy Uncle Sam. But they love it. It took me 22 years to realize we live in the valley. It took me 2.5 months to realize that we live there by choice.

I remember the APA attacking its Soviet counterparts as "barbaric" a few years ago for, among other things, complying with the State's demand that political dissidents be deemed "insane" in order to destroy their credibility and then destroying their minds with a steady stream of psychotropics.

A few days ago, it was my intention to ask you to deliver me from these quack vampires. Now I find it impossible to find the words in any language on earth that would adequately express my utter contempt, disgust, and disillusionment with the whole of humanity.

Do with me what you want. I feel that I no longer possess the capacity to even make the effort to care.

Sincerely,

Marshall R. Ledbetter, Jr.

This text is remarkable for a number of reasons. Although it is a little rough in places, remember that Ledbetter did not have the luxury of revision and multiple drafts. When understood in light of the conditions of its production, most of what Marshall says seems remarkably coherent. It is interesting how he uses the language of redemption to describe his motivations for taking over the capitol. Marshall talks about being patronized and rejected by his family and friends for his beliefs, and betrayed by purported allies who were doing nothing for his freedom. He identifies with 1980s Soviet dissidents dismissed as nutcases and force-fed mind-altering drugs in order to realign them with the party line. Ledbetter also makes a few provocative comments about slavery and freedom. The letter provides a sense of Ledbetter's isolation and unhappiness as well as a lingering suspicion that he might not need to be there. It is not known how Judge Gary reacted to Marshall's letter. One would hope it would have spurred him to look into the status of Ledbetter's case or to ask someone to check on Marshall's welfare. But it is probably just as likely that the note was simply added to Ledbetter's file.

On September 9 the *Tallahassee Democrat* ran a front-page story about Marshall. A sidebar brought uninformed readers up to speed: "Ledbetter tweaked the nose of the establishment by defying high-tech

I stormed the capitol because it was my premise that (I), through individual action, it was still possible to, if not save, then at least help not only oneself, ~~but also~~ one's fellow man. I had already experienced, by their patronization of me and rejection of my beliefs, betrayal not only by my family but also by the vast majority of those I believed my friends. Now, by witnessing firsthand the refusal of those few I considered my allies to undertake any significant, effective action to obtain my release, by seeing them still doing nothing but sitting around getting drunk, waiting impatiently for the massive, inefficient state apparati to (maybe) spit me back out on the street after I have been sufficiently ground up, at which time I will, obviously, somehow help them (because, of course, no matter what he said or how empathically he stated it, it's obviously insane to even believe I could actually save my own soul), I have seen even them deny me.

     Humanity says it hates to live in slavery, in fear, under the velvet-covered iron glove of Sugar Daddy Uncle Sam. But they love it. It took me 22 years to realize we live in the valley. It took me 2.5 months to realize that we live there by choice.

     I remember the APA attacking its Soviet counterparts as "barbaric" a few years ago for, among other things, complying with the State's demand that political dissidents be deemed "insane" in order to destroy their credibility and then destroying their minds with a steady stream of psychotropics. A few days ago it was my intention to ask you to deliver me from these quack vampires. Now I find it impossible to find the words in any language on earth that would adequately express my utter contempt, disgust, and disillusionment with the whole of humanity. Do with me what you want. I truly feel that I no longer possess the capacity to even make the effort to care.

Marshall Ledbetter wrote this letter to Judge William Gary shortly before his brief escape from Florida State Hospital in Chattahoochee in September 1991.

security and holding the sheriff's SWAT team at bay for more than five hours after breaking through the Capitol's glass door with a towel-wrapped whiskey bottle."[31] The main purpose of the article was to report on Ledbetter's continuing refusal to submit to lithium treatment for a mental illness he did not believe he had.

In an interview with the paper, he told them: "Try as I might, I can't get these people to back off. They want to bring me down from one meg to 64 K, so that when I get to court, I'll be dull and bovine. They want to ensure that when I am finally released, I will be a drugged out idiot. I will be counting the roaches on the wall."[32] Ledbetter compared himself to political prisoner Nelson Mandela. He was adamant in his opposition to being medicated against his will. "I will physically resist," he declared. "And when they shove that needle into my arm, I am not going to eat. I am not going to let them steal my soul."[33]

In an interview with the *Flambeau*, Marshall said: "I wouldn't mind them giving me drugs if they were the right drugs. But I intend to physically fight them if they try to administer lithium to me." As he saw it, the authorities were trying to control him: "They don't want your mind to race because they can't keep up. And I don't intend to let them take my mind."[34] From Marshall's perspective, assenting to lithium treatment would be tantamount to admitting that he was "insane at the time."[35] He wasn't willing to make such a concession. "The state is trying to undermine my credibility," he said. "They're trying to mold people into good little ants, into being hive workers. And if people don't stop being behavior modified they're going to get crushed."[36]

At some level, Marshall's antics, rhetoric, and recalcitrance must have been starting to become a thorn in the side of the Florida justice system. A stream of media coverage about anarchist "prisoner of war" Marshall Robin Ledbetter Jr. being held down and injected with lithium by state psychiatrists would not have been welcomed by those in charge. Even some state officials seemed to be on Marshall's side. Shimon Gottschalk, head of the Human Rights Advocacy Committee, a governor-appointed panel created in 1984 to oversee potential abuses of power within Florida's Department of Health and Rehabilitative Services, asked the important question: "What did he do but embarrass the system? And maybe the system deserved it."[37]

Randy Murrell's boss, Nancy Daniels, described the legal dilemma posed by Marshall's situation. "It's difficult for mentally ill patients to know that they need treatment," she said. "The other side of the coin is that it is an invasive procedure in somebody's body, to force it against their will."[38] Ledbetter's mind seemed made up. "I'd prefer not to be treated 'for my own good,'" he said.[39]

Legally, the state of Florida does have the power to medicate its citizens against their will, even when the patient does not acknowledge or agree with the diagnosis. Florida Statute 916.13 grants state hospitals the authority to "retain and treat" defendants determined "incompetent to proceed" for a period lasting no more than six months. According to Stuart Parsons, forensics administrator at Florida State Hospital at the time of Ledbetter's hospitalization, "If a patient committed by the court refuses medication, a petition from the circuit court has the authority to administer medication in spite of whether the patient refuses it."[40]

There is, of course, a legal process that needs to be followed before treatment can commence. In Marshall's case, a hearing was scheduled for October 1991 in Gadsden County to work out the legal issues involved. Marcia Wieder, another attorney working with Marshall, insisted on following proper procedure before an "essential treatment order" would be carried out. "My thought on this is that it's just coercion," she said. "The state's got to jump through some hurdles and I'm going to see that they do. My job is to represent the client's liberty interests, and medication is an intrusion."[41]

Ledbetter's hearing about the legality of an involuntary lithium treatment would never take place. At 7:40 p.m. on September 25, Marshall decided to make a break for it. He tied his jeans, a jacket, and a sheet together and ran toward the east perimeter fence surrounding Unit 23. He scrambled up the eight-foot interior chain-link fence and jumped down the other side. He then threw his makeshift rope over another chain-link fence, this one twelve feet high and topped with razor wire. Marshall pulled himself up using his rope, made it over the razor wire, and jumped down on the other side. Marshall hit the ground hard. He got up running and raced toward Mosquito Creek. After being in custody for a hundred days, Marshall Ledbetter was free.

Recovery

What did this guy do? He didn't hurt anybody. And who's to say what is mental illness? I mean, Joan of Arc heard voices.

Shimon Gottschalk, in Pudlow, "Resistance to Treatment Confounds Doctors, Courts"

It's a relief. . . . They don't think I'm nuts.

Marshall Ledbetter, in Lustig, "Ledbetter Begins Voluntarily Taking Prozac"

Ledbetter's liberty was short-lived. He was captured just moments later. That night he was locked up isolated in the Behavioral Isolation Unit. He continued his vociferous opposition to lithium treatment and told the staff he would commit suicide if he was forcibly medicated. Ledbetter was placed under suicide watch. He was returned to Unit 23 the following day.

In an interview about the escape attempt, Ledbetter said he "managed to make it over the razor wire, but I lost my glasses on the other side. I went in a ditch, over a hill, and then I fell, losing my glasses. I knew it was all over then."[1] *Flambeau* writer Lauren Lustig reported that Marshall "didn't put up any fight when he was caught by two security personnel, and was surprised at how quick they were able to apprehend him."[2] In explaining his reasons for the escape attempt, Marshall said he just felt compelled to break out. "I had to make an effort," he said. "I had to try it. Every day I would have stood there in front of the fence and wondered if I could get out that way. At least now I know."[3] After his capture Marshall was "taken to a main cell, with bars and a toilet, where he tried to get warm all night because he didn't have a blanket." He said he preferred it to his other room at the hospital. "I liked it better. . . . It was a more honest atmosphere."[4]

Marshall offered his thoughts on the legal status of his case. He said that the terms offered by Florida State Hospital as a precondition of his release were unacceptable to him. "I'd have to acknowledge the assertion that what I did was wrong," he said. "In other words: 'you can walk if you sell out.' But now that I've gone up there (to the Capitol), I can't back down."[5]

Ledbetter expressed regret that the break-in at the capitol had not awoken the FSU student body from their slumber. "I figured if I went up to the Capitol and made the cops look like chumps, it might give students some *cojones*," he told Lustig. "But they don't care." Marshall was troubled by the lack of a movement demanding his release. "Every day I wake and realize I missed another sunrise, and every day I wonder if there will be some sort of public outcry on my behalf and every night I go to bed disillusioned. For a while, I was willing to fight. . . . Now all I want to do is go to a mountain range somewhere and be alone."[6]

At the time, the maximum penalty for attempting to escape from a treatment program in Florida was fifteen years in prison. In Marshall's case, however, it might have helped him get out early. After the escape, he was assigned a new treatment team composed of two doctors, a nurse, and a counselor. Suddenly, Marshall made quick and dramatic improvement. The new medical team retracted the lithium treatment order that had been insisted upon before.

Part of the reason for Ledbetter's swift improvement seems to have been a newfound willingness to face certain claims about his mental health. Although he had resisted taking any medication since he was admitted to Chattahoochee, in late October he started taking the antidepressant drug Prozac voluntarily. "I'm doing this by choice," he said. "I started looking at my thought patterns recognizing I was basically going into some serious depressions. . . . I was always high because when I wasn't high, I was feeling shitty."[7]

Ledbetter was facing the reality of his predicament. He said he was looking forward to his release from the hospital so he could face the charges against him. He was no longer triumphalist over what had occurred at the capitol five months earlier. "My life has degraded into a low budget B movie," he said. "If I could find the scriptwriter, I'd fire him."[8]

On November 5, 1991, Robert Alcorn Jr., director of forensic services at the hospital, wrote to the Leon County clerk of the court that Marshall Ledbetter was competent to face the charges against him. Alcorn reminded the court that it had thirty days to review his file and set a hearing. The process initiating Ledbetter's deinstitutionalization had begun. Along with his letter, Alcorn enclosed a seven-page assessment written by Unit 23 senior psychologist Dr. Jill Schwartz.

In her report, Schwartz said that she had met with Ledbetter, reviewed all the relevant documents in his case, and spoken with his mother. Schwartz wrote that since his admittance to Chattahoochee in June, "Mr. Ledbetter has been seen by several psychiatrists in order to clarify his diagnosis. . . . Several diagnoses were offered including Narcissistic Personality, Paranoid Schizophrenia, Schizoaffective Disorder, and a Mood Disorder."[9] Schwartz told the judge that in early October, Marshall's mental state had started to improve dramatically. She said his "presentation of ideas has become more realistic," and he began to "relate to people in more meaningful ways." When questioned about his earlier behavior, Marshall had said he "had still been feeling the effects of the psilocybin."[10] Marshall also told her that "some of his statements were made in jest and he did not realize how seriously they would be taken."[11]

Schwartz explained that the hospital's "Treatment Team withdrew the petition for medication [lithium] because Mr. Ledbetter was not showing signs or symptoms of a formal thought disorder."[12] Marshall was in many respects was a model patient, she said: "Mr. Ledbetter attends Yard, Library, Arts and Crafts, Hortitherapy, Individual Music Therapy, and Music Therapy Group. . . . He has assisted some of the other patients by tutoring them in Competency concepts. He has been attending groups on the unit . . . and has been a meaningful participant. He spends a large portion of his time reading books. Overall, he has been a cooperative patient."[13] Schwartz also mentioned that Marshall had been willingly taking antidepressants.

Getting into the specifics of his cognitive functioning, Schwartz wrote that Marshall "demonstrates no confusion." She said that "The form or structure of Ledbetter's thinking is tight . . . shows no delusions or paranoia." Marshall "does hold some strong viewpoints about world issues and becomes frustrated because others don't agree with him. This frustration is expressed in increasingly pressured speech and statements which convey a naiveté about the world not always being a 'fair' place." The psychologist said Marshall "reported feeling depression because of his circumstances" and "regret about his prior actions." He was "expressing sorrow and regret" about his previous "experiences on drugs" and was "beginning to realize he has had bad trips." She said Ledbetter admitted using "alcohol and drugs as a form of 'escape' from his problems and as a means to 'get in with the crowd.'"[14]

Overall, Schwartz argued, "Mr. Ledbetter does not display deficits in those areas usually considered in determining a defendant's competency to proceed." In her opinion, Marshall did "not require inpatient psychiatric treatment."[15] She offered a treatment plan for the young man: "Once his legal situation is resolved, he will require a system of mental health resources." More specifically, this would necessitate "1. Admission to a residential drug rehabilitation program in order to recover from his substance abuse; 2. Individual therapy in which he focuses on more adaptive ways of coping with issues and problems he is facing; and 3. Family therapy in order to resolve conflicts which have existed since his childhood."[16]

On November 10, five days after the court received Schwartz's statement, former Dead Kennedys lead singer Jello Biafra was in Tallahassee for a performance at The Moon, the largest musical venue in town, on East Lafayette Street. He was delivering material from his newly released spoken-word album, *I Blow Minds for a Living*. At the show, Jello says, some friends of Marshall's appeared and presented him with a photocopy of Ledbetter's demands note.

Biafra remembers, "People at Florida State told me about it. . . . Being a fan of pranks and creative crime, I was intrigued immediately."[17] The celebrity must have learned a little more about Marshall's situation, given the statement he made about Ledbetter that night during his performance. He was discussing the release of political prisoners in the Soviet Union and told the crowd: "Some of them had been force-fed Lithium, like I guess they've been trying to do to Marshall Ledbetter."[18]

On December 11, Judge William Gary issued an order for Marshall to be transported from Chattahoochee to Tallahassee to face the charges against him. A hearing was scheduled in Leon County court for December 19. In an interview with the *Flambeau,* Marshall's attorney, public defender Randy Murrell, offered his thoughts on the case. He said that Ledbetter was "in pretty good health. He had a pretty dramatic change and I think the doctors are right." Murrell was optimistic that his client would be released from the hospital. "I've never had the impression (the prosecution was) out to treat him harshly," he said. "And I think the fact that his mental health has improved will definitely come into consideration."[19]

Judge Gary apparently agreed with this assessment, and after Marshall paid a $5,000 cash bond on January 3, 2002, he granted Marshall a pretrial release. Until his upcoming trial, Ledbetter was to live with his parents in Auburndale, Florida, abide by an 11:00 p.m. curfew, undertake substance-abuse and mental-health counseling, and submit to weekly urine-analysis testing. He was directed to get in contact with his pretrial release officer at least twice a week. Marshall's parents were "ordered to report any violations of these requirements immediately."[20]

During his time spent in Chattahoochee, Marshall underwent a severe reevaluation of his plight. Upon leaving the facility, he no longer considered himself as a political dissident being brainwashed by the state. Instead, he viewed his time in the hospital as a healthy and positive intervention into his mental well-being. Friend Jonathan Lammers explained the gestalt shift that had occurred: "I think that spending six months in a state mental institution accomplished exactly what it was supposed to. He was a karma-quake waiting to happen. It took the slickest psychologists they had to get the wedge into him. . . . Marshall thought he was God, and it's a long way down."[21]

Busted

Big ole nurse all dressed in white
Slaps you on a table in the middle of the night
Then he straps you down real tight
You're wonderin', what'd I do?

Townes van Zandt, "Sanitarium Blues"

I have plainly come to see that '91 was a wasted effort. The only good that came out of it was that I met some cool people in Chattahoochee.

Marshall Ledbetter, "Tales of Psychoboy," September 24, 1996

When Marshall returned to Polk County in January 1992, he was in many ways a changed man. He was repentant and apologetic about what had happened up in Tallahassee six months before. In a follow-up interview with the *Florida Flambeau*, he tried to describe what had happened to him: "I just sort of came down off my trip, you could say. . . . I'm still sort of stunned by the magnitude of everything. It's hard to really explain how I was thinking—really squirrelly."[1]

Marshall's statements are those of a chastened, contrite, and somewhat humiliated individual. He seemed light-years away from the militant activist who had stormed the capitol. In his final story about the capitol incident, Josh Mitchell posed a question on many readers' minds: "Supporters of Ledbetter over the past six months might be asking themselves, 'Is Marshall Ledbetter a broken man? Did the system finally turn him into the "spaced-out cow" that he always feared it would?'"[2]

"Doomed messiah now loves big brother" summed up the attitude of those who answered in the affirmative.[3] For his part, Ledbetter simply claimed he had grown tired of shouldering the burdens of others. "All of those people, you know, somehow wanted me to be their Jesus. . . . Before the whole thing went ballistic, it was like all these people wanted me to sit there and shake my fist at the authorities—why should I let myself be crucified for them?" Marshall said he "could have kept trying to build myself into some sort of hero—but what would it have really done?"[4]

Ledbetter admitted that the break-in was not the best way to draw attention to the issues—such as Native American rights, education, homelessness, and poverty—that animated him. "There would be better avenues, I think, than creating more havoc—which is all I really did," he said. "I'm just someone who dug myself into a really weird hole."[5] Marshall said he occasionally felt "a bit like the Elephant Man" walking around Auburndale.[6] But mainly he just didn't bring it up, assuming—most likely correctly—that local friends and acquaintances would have no clue what he was talking about.[7]

On February 27, Ledbetter traveled back to Tallahassee and entered a plea of *nolo contendere* (no contest) to the charge of second-degree burglary, a felony. The "second degree" designation means that Marshall did "not make an assault or battery nor was he armed with a dangerous weapon or explosive" during the commission of his crime at the capitol.[8] It appears that the prosecution realized there was not enough evidence to consider Ledbetter armed and dangerous during the break-in. Adjudication was withheld, and Ledbetter was placed on probation until March 1997. In his order, Judge Gary declared that Marshall was "not likely again engage in a criminal course of conduct and that the ends of justice and the welfare of society" did not require him to be found guilty.[9]

The charge of criminal mischief and his escape attempt from Chattahoochee were acknowledged and included in the order. Marshall's pending DUI violation curiously disappeared (in Ledbetter's criminal history sheet it is listed as having been turned over to another agency). The maximum sentence for second-degree burglary is five years in prison. Ledbetter was sentenced to five years of probation concurrent with the sentence. He was charged $2,200 in fines and had to pay $40 a month to the State of Florida to defray the costs of his probation.

The conditions of Ledbetter's probation were strict, just like those of his pretrial release order. He still had an 11:00 p.m. curfew, and he could not move, change jobs, or travel outside Polk County "without first procuring the written consent of [his] Probation Officer." Marshall was not allowed to carry a firearm, violate any law, "use intoxicants to excess, nor . . . visit places where intoxicants, drugs or other dangerous substances are unlawfully sold, dispensed or used." He was ordered to "undergo mental screening and substance abuse screening."[10]

Judge Gary banged his gavel and sent Ledbetter on his way. This crazy, twisted chapter in Marshall's life had finally come to an end. He was now living back in the family home in Auburndale, taking antidepressants, working at Marshall's Camera, tooling around on his bicycle, and getting back into the rhythms of Polk County life. All things considered, it was a soft landing for the young man who not long before had the full firepower of a SWAT team pointed in his direction.

As far as his future was concerned, Marshall said he wanted to go back to school and finish his bachelor's degree, but he wasn't sure where. Florida State University was out of the question for obvious reasons, not the least of which was the $900 in fines he owed Strozier Library.[11] So for the time being Marshall lived with his parents and worked for the family business. It seems most of the time he adhered to the conditions of his probation, but he would occasionally violate them. On one occasion he snuck out of town with his brother, Arlen, and a few other friends for a night of drinking and carousing at Sweeny Todd's on Church Street in Orlando. Marshall was buying the rounds that night and spent $83 on drinks for the party of five over the course of the evening. Everyone had a great time until Marshall vomited in the armrest on the way home.[12]

About two years passed, and then in May 1994, Marshall unfortunately got in serious trouble once again. Bert Peppe was undergoing radiation treatment for Hodgkin's disease up in Tallahassee. His days were possibly numbered, and Marshall wanted to see him. On May 11, Ledbetter telephoned his probation officer, Marlon Mizelle, and asked for permission to travel to the capital to visit his ill friend. Mizelle instructed Marshall to "bring in the name, address and itinerary of where he would be staying in Tallahassee and obtain a written travel permit."[13]

Ledbetter had been meaning to visit Tallahassee for about a week and was desperate to get out of town. On the morning of May 13, he was working at Marshall's camera. "This woman came in and started complaining about her photos or something," Marshall said. "I just couldn't handle it, I left the store, I walked to the bus station and got on the bus."[14] This alarmed Marshall's father, who called Mizelle and told him that Marshall was on a bus to Tallahassee. He said he was "acting extremely bizarre" and might be "capable of irrational behavior."[15]

Mizelle called up to Ocala and arranged to have deputies detain Ledbetter when the bus pulled in for a pit stop en route to the capital. Marshall was arrested for violating his probation while standing in front of a snack machine, contemplating his options.[16] "It was a set up," Marshall declared. "There were cops all over the bus station."[17]

Ledbetter now faced new criminal charges in addition to the ones associated with the break-in: leaving Polk County without written permission and failing to follow instructions. Mizelle also suggested that Marshall "be re-evaluated for mental health counseling."[18] Ledbetter was taken from the Ocala bus station to a nearby detention center. He was held there in solitary confinement for the next eight days. To make matters worse, Marshall had apparently ingested "approximately one half tab of LSD just prior to his arrest."[19] This means it is quite likely he was still under the effects of the psychedelic drug when he was apprehended and put in solitary confinement. As someone like Timothy Leary would be the first to tell you, being in solitary confinement in a detention center would be the worst possible environment for an acid trip.

Marshall would later tell a psychological examiner that he "could not understand why he was isolated."[20] The arresting officers would have been well aware of who Marshall Ledbetter was and what had occurred at the capitol back in 1991. They would have been skeptical of his claim to be simply traveling to Tallahassee to visit a friend who might be dying.

After spending more than a week in isolation, Ledbetter was transported from Ocala to the Leon County jail. He spent five days in that facility before being "Baker Acted" and placed once again under the care of the state. Public defender Randy Murrell represented him once again and filed a "motion to determine competency to proceed." In stark, chilling language, the document outlined Marshall's disintegration. "According to nurses at the jail," Murrell wrote, "the defendant is suicidal, has at one time or another torn off his clothes, and is out of control. . . . The defendant is in need of immediate psychiatric or psychological care."[21] Marshall was moved from the Leon County jail to the PATH (Positive Alternative to Hospitalization) Crisis Stabilization Unit at the Apalachee Center in Tallahassee.[22]

Ledbetter underwent a psychological examination at PATH on May 27, 1994. Coincidentally, he was screened once again by Dr. William E. Spence, the same psychologist who had evaluated him twice in the weeks after the capitol incident and who had recommended his institutionalization at Chattahoochee. Marshall, who had been at the PATH facility for three days, was wearing "a hospital gown, jeans and bedroom slippers" when he met the psychologist. None of the bravado, wit, or irony he had expressed after the capitol break-in was now evident in Marshall's demeanor. The examiner asked Ledbetter if he remembered him. Marshall replied, "I remember you Dr. Spence, sometimes, I don't know, I would like to go in the other room and eat breakfast with my friends, they are all my friends here."[23]

Spence observed that Marshall "looked rather disheveled and perplexed." Although Marshall denied being suicidal or homicidal, Spence said he seemed anxious. He was "tearful during the interview at times and his affect was flat on occasion [and] appropriate to depression."[24] Marshall "denied current hallucinations or illusions" and "did not appear to be paranoid or delusional." Marshall "described past feelings of racing thoughts, of wanting to give items away . . . [of] wanting to visit an Indian Reservation and [wanting to] 'help the world.'" Spence said that Ledbetter, while "cooperative . . . was somewhat grandiose at times . . . was loose, tangential and circumstantial on occasion" and "had difficulty at times getting to the point in responding to questions."[25]

A good chunk of the assessment focused on Marshall's drug and alcohol use, which had persisted despite his being on probation. "Ledbetter related that he has continued to use alcohol and drugs," Spence wrote. "He has used marijuana, ranging from two or three cigarettes a week to an ounce every three days. He has used LSD when he could 'find it.' . . . He has 'used mushrooms' and also experimented with ecstasy, called X. . . . Mr. Ledbetter's abuse of alcohol and drugs has increased over a six month period. Mr. Ledbetter reported that he had been stressed out for an extended period of time."[26]

Marshall told Spence that he "had no idea why he was in PATH."[27] When asked about his plans for the future, Ledbetter replied: "I'm going to sell all my CDs, all of them. I'm going to go to a store and buy some camping equipment. I'm going to the mountains of North Carolina to find an Indian tribe, the Cherokee. My mother's, mother's mother or something like that was Cherokee. Maybe I can live with them and get away from all this. I've had it with these people around me."[28]

Ledbetter was being truthful regarding his ancestry. According to his mother, "Marshall's maternal great-great-great-grandmother was said to be Cherokee. At family reunions there were discussions of family heritage while sharing family genealogy charts." She continues: "I do remember Marshall asking about this when he was in high school. I told him, according to uncles and cousins, his maternal side had some Cherokee lineage."[29]

As part of the assessment, Spence spoke to Marshall's father. Marshall had been acting strangely and losing weight, his father said. At first he thought it was just because Marshall was spending so much time on his bicycle—his only form of transportation—but now he wasn't sure. Marshall "would have periods of time when he was outgoing and verbal and other times when he would withdraw."[30] In Spence's view, Marshall was in no condition to face the charges against him. Ledbetter was "out of touch with reality at this time and is incompetent to proceed."

Spence said that Marshall "presents himself as being a Bipolar

Disorder, Manic Type, and is also seen as 'coming down' or withdrawing from hallucinogenic drugs."[31] He said that Ledbetter would not be well served in the Leon County jail. He needed "a period of time to be able to appropriately test reality," preferably "in a structured, hospital setting." Spence predicted that Marshall would "improve in time, with medication, observation and treatment."[32]

A week went by, and on June 4 another psychologist, Dr. Harry A. McClaren, evaluated Ledbetter's competency for the court. Still at PATH, Marshall was brought to the examination room in restraints, which were removed before the assessment. In his report to Judge Nikki Clark, who was now presiding over the case, McClaren wrote, "During all contacts with Mr. Ledbetter, he presented as a frankly psychotic person most likely suffering from Schizoaffective disorder."[33] McClaren noted that Ledbetter was experiencing "suicidal ideation and behavior" and was considered an "intermittent suicide risk." In addition, Ledbetter "had been physically assaultive to PATH staff."[34] Marshall's "activity level was excessive and he appeared anxious at times. At other times he appeared rather euphoric. He was quite emotionally unstable as at times he appeared depressed and close to tears."[35] Ledbetter had "little insight into his mental difficulties saying that he did not believe that he suffered from a mental illness at one point. At another point he said that he believed that he suffered from a Manic Depressive illness . . . [or] that he might have Alzheimer's disease. At one point when near tears he advised 'ever since I did those mushrooms in 1991 . . . I can't figure out how to get out of here.'"

According to McClaren, Marshall "appeared to have a grossly intact memory. While his speech was understandable, he showed definite flight of ideas and rambling speech. At times he was quite circumstantial and tangential. Most likely he was suffering from delusions involving persecution. For example, he talked about believing that people were staring into his eyes trying to read his thoughts. Grandiosity was in evidence as he talked about how he believed that he was going to send rap albums out in a professional manner."[36] McClaren said that since Marshall was "combative at times and in need of physical restraints despite aggressive chemotherapy, he appears in need of more long-term inpatient psychiatric care." Not institutionalizing Ledbetter would increase the risk of his being "a danger to himself, and the potential for dangerousness towards others seems above average as well."[37]

On June 22, Randy Murrell filed a motion waiving Marshall's right to a competency hearing. It was approved by Judge Clark. Both examiners had concluded that Ledbetter was "incompetent to proceed and should be committed to Florida State Hospital for further treatment." Murrell wrote: "Rather than incur any further delay, the defendant is willing to waive a hearing and requests this Court to make its determination of the defendant's competency to proceed based solely on the written reports."[38] Marshall would soon be heading back to Chattahoochee.

We know a lot less about how Marshall fared during his second visit to Florida State Hospital, but there are a few anecdotes. Marshall managed to make a number of telephone calls to Dr. Walter Tschinkel, his biology professor from Florida State University. Tschinkel says it sounded like Ledbetter was on very heavy medication and that Marshall kept making references to outer space. Tschinkel was concerned. After their third conversation, he contacted staff at Chattahoochee and alerted them to what was going on. He told them it "probably wasn't a good idea" for one of their patients to be communicating with him so frequently.[39]

The calls to Tschinkel stopped, but not before Ledbetter managed to communicate with at least two other individuals. One person Marshall reached out to was *Tallahassee Democrat* reporter Mark Hinson. Ledbetter called him at odd hours, leaving rambling messages about "weird stuff."[40] From what Hinson could gather, Marshall seemed to be saying that he was being held against his will at the hospital and was not cooperating with the staff.[41] When Hinson managed to get Ledbetter on the phone, Marshall was subdued and uncommunicative. He quietly told the reporter he didn't have anything to say and hung up.

Hinson's fellow *Democrat* staff writer Steve MacQueen also heard from Marshall. He remembers it being "not a happy phone call" and that Marshall was "talking slow." A few moments into the conversation,

MacQueen heard a siren in the background through the phone and what sounded like a riot breaking out. Ledbetter told him, "I think I have to go," and ended the call.[42]

One way or another, Marshall successfully completed his second tour of Florida State Hospital. On December 16, hospital director Steve W. Collins sent a letter to Judge Clark, informing the court that Ledbetter was now competent to face the charges against him. A month later, Marshall was released from the hospital and returned to the Leon County jail. On January 25, 1995, Judge Clark signed an order modifying Marshall's sentence. It had been almost three years since he was initially placed on probation. Ledbetter had disobeyed the orders of the court through his unapproved bus trip to Tallahassee. Because of the violation, he was now judged guilty of second-degree burglary. Marshall was given credit for the 254 days he had been incarcerated, but he would remain on probation for another two years. He was ordered to "take whatever psychotropic medication that is prescribed to him" and to "participate in mental health counseling and substance abuse counseling."[43] Ledbetter was given a bill for $200 in public defender services and released into the custody of his father.

"Tales of Psychoboy"

If your I.Q. is over 150, and you have $3125.00 (plus hand-ling), you might be eligible for a trial membership in the Ancient Illuminated Seers of Bavaria. If you think you qualify, put the money in a cigar box and bury it in your backyard. One of our Underground Agents will contact you shortly.

Ravenhurst, *Principia Discordia*

I've decided to create a weekly newsletter detailing my activities in Polk County, not only for my friends who have escaped, but also for those fortunate enough not to have had to survive in this fetid rat-hole.

Marshall Ledbetter, "Tales of Psychoboy," August 17, 1996

Marshall was back in Auburndale. For reasons that were partially re-lated to their eldest son's difficulties, his parents had divorced in 1993. Marshall Sr. had bought out Sharon's share of the business. Marshall lived with his father in the family home and continued to work at Mar-shall's Camera. Sharon says that on his good days, Marshall Jr. was excellent with the customers, teaching and educating them about the products and how to work the equipment.

Marshall renewed his relationship with Cate Stoecklin, who was still living in Tallahassee. They saw each other when they could and main-tained a vigorous letter-writing correspondence. Tallahassee resident and FSU alum Charla Renker,[1] who knew Stoecklin socially in the mid-1990s, remembers her as a "brilliant engineer who had her ups and downs." Occasionally, Marshall would visit Cate in Tallahassee. Renker remembers spotting Marshall and Cate renting movies together at the Blockbuster on Apalachee Parkway. Deon Gondron,[2] a friend from Landis Hall who knew Marshall while he lived in Tallahasee, says they "were essentially two nerdy people, well matched for each other. She was obviously smart and could relate to Marshall intellectually. I think she thought Marshall was essentially a sweet guy with some charming quirks."[3] Unfortunately, the relationship would not last. Before long, Stoecklin broke up with him.[4]

Ledbetter's connections to Tallahassee were now slipping almost completely away. His Landis Hall roommate Fritz Krawchuk, one of the few friends from Florida State to keep in contact with Marshall during this time, says "life was kind of sad" for Ledbetter. He "clocked his hours at the camera shop," doing "a little bit of everything," but the impression he got when he visited Marshall in Auburndale in 1995 was that Ledbetter was simply bored. "For someone as academically gifted as he was, it must have been killing him he didn't have an outlet."[5]

One outlet that Marshall did find was to publish, in the fall of 1996, a journal of sorts called "Tales of Psychoboy." This was a very informal magazine project, written for a small group of friends, family members, and acquaintances. It was basically a diary of Marshall's life at this point in time. In some entries, Marshall pieced together news clippings with advertisements of varied significance, adding his doodles and ironic comments. Mainly, though, Ledbetter just wrote about his quotidian existence. He spills a lot of ink discussing the local coffee shop, eating and hanging out with friends at various bars and restaurants, zipping around Polk County on his mountain bike.

Ledbetter became politically active after returning to Polk County. He volunteered for the local Democratic Party. Marshall discusses going to a political event in August 1996 to "take pictures of Mike Canady (D)—House District #23—as he glad-hands thousands of Plant City rednecks attending a rally for hometown hero swimmer/gold medalist Brooke Bennett."[6] Three days later, Ledbetter abruptly switched political allegiance to do some phone canvassing for the Republicans, since "those lukewarm Demo. Liberals had been getting on my nerves." He said he "felt like George Blake"[7]—the famous British double agent—"playing both sides of the line."[8]

The next day Marshall arrived back at Winter Haven's Democratic Headquarters. The higher-ups, a "self-appointed tribunal of two," were acting funny and had something to say to him. As it turned out, it had nothing—as he had feared—to do with the phone canvassing for the Republicans, but rather Ledbetter's break-in at the capitol five years earlier. They had learned what he had done. Marshall was declared unfit for the Democratic Party. "Given your past history, we feel that your continued presence at headquarters would not be conducive to the image we are trying to project," they said.[9] Marshall "laughed sardonically and left" the building.[10]

The following day, Ledbetter tells us, he was approached by a Mr. Brumbaugh, member of the Lake Alfred chapter of the Democratic Party. He told Marshall that the Winter Haven Democrats had "overstepped their bounds."[11] Brumbaugh wanted Marshall to accompany him and his wife to the Lakeland Democratic Executive Meeting that very evening to straighten things out. Marshall notes, "Apparently I am a pawn in some internecine power struggle. I smile gleefully and accept." Ledbetter said he would be happy to explain the extent of "Stalinist behavior" in the Winter Haven branch, how its leaders were out to "stifle dissent" and trying to "bring the party cadre under their direct control."[12]

In spite of a few such intriguing tales, however, most of the events and experiences that Marshall Ledbetter chronicles in "Tales of Psychoboy" are fairly mundane. He writes at length about working at his dad's camera shop, developing film, eating oysters, drinking beer, going to parties, playing chess, going to the IHOP, watching a ballet, and attending jam sessions where he would occasionally rap lyrics along with the music.

Marshall discusses wanting to form a band named Yudhisthira's Dog but laments, "The only problem is that no one down here has their shit together. Their either drunkards or meth-freaks or smack junkies."[13] He describes hanging out with his brother, Arlen, throwing Frisbee, buying beer for underaged friends, taking care of a stray dalmatian, giving his pager number to "an all-around excellent, funny, funny girl" named Jill,[14] the acting talents of Clint Eastwood, and going to the movies.

Marshall discusses a court-ordered therapy session with his "Happy Hindu Shrink"—a certain Dr. Pandya. The psychiatrist tells Ledbetter he "must make some money to be happy, as that seems to be what greases the wheels in all of these societies."[15] Marshall describes listening to music and reading a lot. A trip to a bookstore might yield a "special order of Trotsky's *My Life* . . . a couple of sci-fi novels, a book on fuzzy logic, some Russian language guides, a biography of [Ervin] Rommel" (the German field marshal implicated in the plot against Hitler), and a copy of *American Scientist* magazine.

In September 1996, Marshall talks about drinking beer late into the night at the Third Street Bar and Grill (later to become Jessie's) "discussing WWI artillery and quantum physics with an ex-biker from Oklahoma." He writes: "Some ball-cap boy offers to buy us a beer if we'll stop talking about stuff he doesn't understand, and the biker tells him to shut up and go crack some books. The kid slinks off. The biker and I head down to Denny's and rap until 5:30 a.m."[16]

Yet not all was well in Marshall's world. "Tales of Psychoboy" juxtaposed stories of an upbeat, frenetic Marshall—he would often refer to himself as "The Happy Hominid"—carousing around Polk County with darker prose reflective of a more despondent figure.[17] He talks about being considerably in debt, and at one point mentions owing the "scumdogs at Winter Haven Hospital, Inc." five thousand dollars for a week of drug and alcohol rehabilitation. "5K for one week," Ledbetter grumbles. "I should've just checked into the Hilton."[18]

He directs a considerable amount of criticism toward the stifling culture of central Florida and the inanities of American society. Ledbetter complains of people who spend "Yet another damn night crawling into a succession of beer bottles instead of engaging in moral, physical and intellectual development. Whether they're drinking Anheuser-Busch product in Imperial Polk County, or shaking their sold-as-product asses on 'The Grind' on MTV, our youth of today are pathetic."[19]

Marshall felt suffocated in Polk County and minced no words making known his displeasure for the place, especially relative to his days at Florida State. He wrote: "I miss the FSU / Monarchy Party Da(ys/ze). . . . Here I am alone. There is no one to talk to. No one who understands. No one who thinks. No one who cares. . . . I am exiled to this place of madness, filled with 'croaking redneck scum.' . . . I'd rather be back in Chattahoochee smoking Buglers with the other state-certified psychopaths."[20]

In late-December 1996, Ledbetter admitted to his friends he had "been attempting to lay off the booze since I tend not to get anything significant accomplished when I am around it." He found giving up alcohol difficult, though, since "the people here that I know who think the most, tend to drink the most."[21] Marshall shared a recurring nightmare about smoking marijuana and getting busted for a faulty urine test: "HONK-HONK-WAAUUGH-WAAUUGH-MARSHALL WHAT THE HELL DID YOU JUST DO YOU'RE GOING TO BE PISS TESTED AND YOU JUST TOKED ON A JOINT WHAT THE FUCK WERE YOU THINKING, etc. etc." Marshall laments: "The State of Florida has even invaded my dreams and I am pissed."[22]

Although Marshall wrote "Tales of Psychoboy" mainly for the edification of his old Tallahassee friends and family members, San Francisco–based punk rocker and political activist Jello Biafra was also on the mailing list. As we have seen, Biafra had had a formative influence on Marshall. Biafra had been listed in Marshall's demands note. Now he was going to throw Ledbetter a bone by recording a song about him. It was called "The Ballad of Marshall Ledbetter."

When asked in 2013 about his motivations for recording the song, Biafra said, "It was such an amazing incident, I just thought I should."[23] Biafra wrote the lyrics for "The Ballad of Marshall Ledbetter" and recorded it with an outfit called Lard, his main band at the time. The band included Al Jourgensen and Paul Barker from the industrial rock group Ministry.

Biafra says that in the course of making the song, he felt he had to reach out to Marshall. "It got to a point where I needed to get his permission to do the song, not legally, but ethically," Biafra said. He called Ledbetter in Auburndale in 1995 or 1996. Jello and Marshall discussed Biafra's idea about the song, and he says Marshall was "OK with it."[24]

The result is a curious musical representation of Ledbetter's capitol showdown delivered through Biafra's nasally screams, Jourgensen's metal guitar, Barker's bass lines, and punishing drumbeats. The most meaningful lines in the song are "I was a prisoner for twenty-two years / When I broke through that door, I was free."

In a 1996 interview, Biafra discussed the context behind the song. "It's about a guy in Florida who seized the Capitol building after breaking in an unguarded front door. . . . He demanded to speak with, among other people, Chuck D, Timothy Leary, Ice Cube, Lemmy, and me. This is an actual story. . . . I have spoken with him. . . . He was somebody who had had enough of the injustice in our world and chose to do something about it in very colorful fashion. I've been a long-time fan of creative crime. The best part about this one is, it made a statement, it was a work of art, and not a single person got hurt."[25]

Although "The Ballad of Marshall Ledbetter" was initially intended for release on the 1997 Lard album, *Pure Chewing Satisfaction*, it didn't appear until February 1, 2000, on the three-track Lard EP, '*70s Rock Must Die*. Biafra says there "wasn't room on *Pure Chewing Satisfaction*. . . . Sure if we had made it a double LP or a long CD, but I prefer my music albums lean and mean."[26]

While Marshall was waiting for the song to be released, his old friends from Tallahassee were moving on with their lives in an upwardly mobile kind of way. They were turning out to be a successful bunch, and many were getting established in careers like banking, law, and education. Fritz Krawchuk visited Marshall in Auburndale. They toured the camera shop and drove around town. They went to a couple of parties and met some of Marshall's friends. Although Ledbetter was in many ways the same warm, funny, intelligent friend he had always been, Krawchuk thought Marshall "didn't look as happy or as vibrant as he had been."[27]

In the summer of 1996, Marshall became involved with a woman named Alicia Calandra. They dated for a very intense six weeks, spending nearly all day in each other's company. "I thought he was great," says Calandra. "Marshall was a fun person."[28] She remembers that Marshall had a strange routine of drinking a beer in the morning while smoking a cigar and reading the newspaper. She also said he thought it funny to "reverse" his medication and take his prescribed pills at the wrong time of day (for example, sedatives in the morning and stimulants at night).[29]

Calandra remembers Ledbetter listening to "a recording of his voice from [his] FSU days, and a classmate was playing a cello in the background. He played that a lot. He also would read the paper from what all happened at FSU, and he would either get really excited and happy or cry. Most of the time [he was] happy, though."[30] Yet before long, Calandra became bothered by Marshall's persistent references to a "girl named Cate."[31] She was hurt when she went to Marshall's house one day and overheard him telling his father that he was planning to break things off with her. Their relationship fizzled out, but not before they produced a child together. Livia Ledbetter was born in May 1997.

Calandra admits, in retrospect, that Marshall "didn't treat me too well." In "Tales of Psychoboy" she gets brief mention as Ledbetter's "ex-girlfriend/Glenn Close nightmare." Marshall describes jumping from bar to bar one evening in Winter Haven "in a vain attempt to evade and escape" her.[32] He showed no interest in an early ultrasound picture presented to him, and he was not present at his daughter's birth. After Livia was born, Marshall paid $211 per month in child support, but otherwise he played no fatherly role at all. Calandra laments that she just "wanted him to see her, [but] he never did."[33] Today, Livia Ledbetter has no memory of Marshall. The last time she saw him, they tell her, was when she was about three years old and was taken for a visit to her grandfather's house. Marshall wasn't in a mood to hang out, so he told Calandra he was tired and cut the visit short. Marshall "wasn't the type who dealt well with responsibility," explains Winter Haven friend Conrad Arbaugh.[34]

In spite of his troubles, Marshall was well known and well liked throughout the community. Arbaugh describes him as a "good guy" who "had all kinds of friends on all kinds of levels."[35] "Girls liked him, everybody liked him; he could and would talk to anybody."[36] Whether by choice or out of necessity, Ledbetter's primary mode of transportation was his mountain bike. Often he would ride to the camera shop in Auburndale, bike the five miles to Winter Haven to drink and play chess, and then pedal back to Auburndale to spend the night.

Sometimes he made this circuit this twice a day, often in the hot, humid, and unpredictable Florida weather.

Because he was constantly on the go, Ledbetter brought his backpack with him everywhere he went. It was filled to the gills with his camera and film, books, magazines, tabloid newspapers, and marijuana and rolling papers. He would make the rounds visiting friends. Marshall would get off his bike to hang out, open up his backpack, and its contents would simply explode all around him.

While Ledbetter's life might not seem too abysmal, relative to his peers and his own aspirations he might have been accused of slumming. Now approaching thirty, he was still basically living like a college student. He eked together a living by working at the camera shop and collecting Social Security disability benefits for his mental illness.[37] Ledbetter probably thought it entirely appropriate that if the government wanted to force a label of mental illness upon him, he might as well get compensated for it. Ledbetter still loved his rap, classic rock, and punk music and continued to express good-natured disdain for hippies.[38] He liked to listen to Drew Garabo's raucous talk show from midnight to 6:00 a.m. on FM 104.1 out of Cocoa Beach. Marshall was an avid NASCAR fan and enjoyed watching professional wrestling on television. He would get together with Conrad Arbaugh, drink beer, and root for the jabroni.

16

Al-Qaeda and the Blue Key Club

You a fast monkey, son? We've got some chemicals for that. Slow your ass down quick and we've got a needle and a cinder block cell if you don't want to 'cooperate' and we'll charge you for our wonderful services, too, so whaddya say, eh? Just take your pills.

Marshall Ledbetter, "Tales of Psychoboy," September 14, 1996

The history books are about meaningless public events like wars and elections and revolutions. The only important things happen in the bodies and brains of individuals, you understand. That's the great secret of human life that scientists never talk about.

Neal Cassady, in Leary, *Flashbacks*

The good times were not to last. Whatever mental-health issues Marshall experienced in the early 1990s were nothing compared to those he would face later in life. Ledbetter's days in Chattahoochee would not be the only ones he would spend in a psychiatric hospital. Indeed, he was committed to one of them—most likely G. Pierce Wood Memorial Hospital in Arcadia—when he got the attention of the authorities yet again.

G. Pierce Wood Memorial Hospital is located seventy miles south of Auburndale. It opened in 1947 on land formerly known as Calstrom Field, a pilot-training facility during World Wars I and II. The hospital is named after Florida's Speaker of the House of Representatives in the late 1930s. The hospital, which at its peak had twelve hundred beds,[1] had been a source of controversy for the state since at least 1987, when the American Civil Liberties Union filed a class-action lawsuit against it. The suit claimed that hundreds of residents at the facility were "needlessly sedated and denied adequate treatment, nutrition and recreation."[2] In 1989, federal inspectors found compelling evidence to substantiate these claims, even after providing the hospital two months' advance notice of their visit. In particular, investigators found elderly patients strapped to chairs all day long and residents "who were not mentally ill nevertheless were being locked in wards with violent, irrational patients and given disabling tranquilizers."[3]

G. Pierce Wood hospital staff were found sleeping on the job, filling out false reports, giving patients the wrong medication, and putting them to bed at 6:00 p.m. The federal inspectors estimated that over 20 percent of the patients did not need to be there. Some female residents were not issued undergarments, and "others were exposed to the stares of men patients while undressing and lining up for the shower." Staff dehumanized the patients and described feeding them as giving "slop to the hogs."[4] Based on the data collected from this report, the federal government placed the hospital under special monitoring and demanded that patients be given more "freedom of movement, quicker discharge and more input into their own treatment plans."[5]

Due to health privacy laws, we don't know when exactly Ledbetter was sent to G. Pierce Wood, why he was there, or how many visits he made to the hospital. But it appears that he was inside the institution in 1998, when he managed to call a reporter with the *Lakeland Ledger* named Joy Murphy. According to the Florida Department of Law Enforcement (FDLE), Ledbetter left the journalist a number of strange phone messages. The communications were "directed towards then Governor Lawton Chiles." In one message in particular, Marshall wanted the newspaper reporter to tell "the governor that he wanted to be released from a mental hospital or members of the University of Florida Blue Key Club would be in danger and be 'terminated.'"[6]

On February 1, 2000, Marshall attracted the attention of special agents with the FDLE yet again. They had been alerted when Ledbetter showed up at the Winter Haven Police Department claiming "he had drugs on him, and that they were poisoning his body." Marshall was searched by an officer on duty, but no drugs were found. A special agent contacted the police station and gave them "information regarding family contacts for Ledbetter."[7] No further action was taken.

In August 2001, Marshall launched a website called marshallledbetter.com. He used it as a way to resurrect the spirit of the witty diatribes and rants he had been known for during his college days. The website was fairly primitive by today's standards. It contained links to an encyclopedia on culture jamming[8] and to information about Ohio-based rapper Pimp Daddy Welfare.[9] There were references to Lard's "Ballad of Marshall Ledbetter" and quotes about the song and Marshall from Jello Biafra.

Marshall wrote and uploaded sixteen rants on his website between August 4, 2001, and March 21, 2002.[10] In chronological order, they are titled "What Would Jesus Drink?" (August 4, 2001), "DOC TV" (August 15, 2001) "Patrick Buchanan Was Right" (August 19, 2001), "Flossing" (October 8, 2001), "Noise" (September 2, 2001), "ACID" (September 9, 2001), "On the Road" (September 19, 2001), "An Amalgamation of Unrelated and Unexpurgated Railings" (September 28, 2001), "Advice for Aspiring Messiahs" (October 17, 2001), "Full-On Drunk Rant" (October 21, 2001), "Thoughts on Renovating Winter Haven" (November 2, 2001), "11-17-01," "11-30-01," "Arcadia" (February 5, 2002), "3-08-02," and "The Al Aqsa Martyrs' Brigade" (March 21, 2002). Today, most of the content from the website is no longer publicly available.[11]

As may be seen by the titles of the rants, Marshall created some of his posts while he was high on various substances. Even so, many of them offer at times cogent and thoughtful insights into the world. The subject matter in these posts ranges from the trivial to the tragic, covering all sorts of topics like religion, politics, education, and how society treats the mentally ill.

One post that provides some perspective on how Ledbetter was living in the early 2000s, "Full-On Rant," begins with a tale about his roommate's cat and its punishment for waking up a hung-over Marshall Ledbetter too early in the morning. Marshall put the cat in the shower. Now that Marshall was awake, he decided to crack a beer and watch the NASCAR race. Marshall's love of NASCAR might seem a little lowbrow given some his other intellectual interests, like chess or Dostoyevsky, but it was a real passion for him.

"NFL players are faggots compared to NASCAR drivers," Ledbetter would claim. "Sure, they'll occasionally drag out the inspiring-to-his-teammates wheelchair-bound result of last season's unfortunate hit, but they're not going 190 mph, five wide. Pussies."[12] The race that afternoon was at Talladega, Alabama. Marshall called it the "death track" because of all the casualties the race had generated over the years, many caused by the severe incline on the curves. "One day someone's ticket's gonna be punched," Marshall said eagerly, "and my video vulture ass will be there to watch it."[13]

In addition to discussing his tastes in television, Marshall used his website to explore more weighty topics such as "the nature of will itself." In "Flossing" he writes that will is "praised as a virtue, scanned for in the students (if not encouraged) by the 'teachers'/ 'overseers'—and channeled by them.[14] . . . Will is seductive and rarely questioned. . . . It's just accepted 'Right or wrong, at least he's ambitious. Nothing wrong with attempting to define other's realities. We'd all do it if we could. . . . He has a long future of imposing his will upon others ahead of him.'"[15] To illustrate his point, Ledbetter mentions Shelley's poem "Ozymandias." In a statement that may indicate just how much influence his time in psychiatric hospitals had upon his sense of personal identity, Marshall says: "I wanted to be Ozymandias too, until I went to Chattahoochee. Then I realized that the Ozymandiases of the world built the Chattahoochees of the world. So fuck it. I took a walk. Try it sometime. You've still got time."[16] Marshall then goes on to describe how power is a worse drug than crack. "Ask any physician," he argues. "Alpha males who perceive themselves to be imposing their will on others register a much higher level of testosterone in their bloodstream. They're powerful and horny . . . fascist control junkies."[17]

The rant "Advice for Aspiring Messiahs" is important for a number of reasons. Here, Marshall reflects on his vision quest and the occupation of the State Capitol Building. It is noteworthy that he frames these experiences in religious terms, casting himself as a latter-day prophet. Ledbetter writes: "Religion is a much heavier gig than politics. The bar's a lot higher. Anyone can publically check off their positions on the current issues laundry list, gain corporate funding, and briefly become Caesar. Interpreting the 'Will of God' is a much murkier business."

After considering the question of monotheism, how to describe the Supreme Being ("Should it be Sentience itself?"), and the nature and extent of this new religion's commandments, Ledbetter admits that these are all "perplexing" issues. He quips, "Things would be a lot easier if a burning bush showed up for consulting purposes."

Marshall continues the rant by discussing the realities of messianic action. He writes: "At one point . . . I thought I even had Moses beat with my ACID acronym from my List of Demands back during the '91 Capitol bit. Annihilate Conditioning Integrate Data. I thought that was pretty damn hot. I would have stacked that up against the Ten Commandments any day of the week. I was so succinct, I thought Sentience itself had to be responsible. Fortunately, ACID never caught on with the public, thus relieving me of any further duties to Sentience."[18]

Ledbetter then launches into a lengthy aside on "Sentience" that also provides insight into why he broke into and occupied the capitol that day:

Yeah, screw you, Sentience! I delivered your message—if it didn't stand on its own two feet that's your fault, not mine. That's what you get for trying to turn religion into a four letter word. Whaddya want me to do, sit around in a library for a few years trying to knock out some exegesis, like Philip K. Dick did before you scrambled him? What? Huh? Don't give me that "You applied for the job during your vision quest," crap. I was just tripping and trying to figure out what to do with my life, and you show up and try to commandeer it. Fuck you. We're even. I'm done. Stop trying to creep around the edges of my consciousness. I'll file a harassment charge. . . . What's that? It's hypocrisy for an anarchist to go to the law? Maybe so, but you're pushing it. Huh? Psych evaluation? ("God's been harassing you again, Ledbetter?") (snicker) "No, not God, Sentience!" (sigh) Whatever. Just start filling out these forms and don't forget to give me your belt and shoelaces. We both know the drill. I'll go break you out a toothbrush.[19]

This rant is notable for a number of reasons. It provides an excellent example of Ledbetter's gifts as a writer, his wry sense of humor, and the multidimensionality of his thought. We are also given the most parsimonious explanation of why Marshall stormed the capitol that summer morning back in June 1991. He says he was "just tripping and trying to figure out what to do with my life."

Continuing with his "advice for aspiring messiahs," Ledbetter makes some suggestive remarks about drugs as a vehicle for religious or mystical experience. Marshall writes that although "hallucinogens can provide this," he warns they are stigmatized by the public, can "shatter the mind for a good stretch," and can cause a "500 mph, introspective meltdown."

"Don't do them if you're afraid of where you might end up," he cautions. "Seeing 'the face of God' should necessarily destroy one and demand a period of re-integration. . . . Buddha—Jesus—Mohammed—Geronimo—would have understood this. The local pastor/sheriff/family member/psychiatrist/judge/friend/employer may or may not."[20]

Marshall was obviously speaking from personal experience here. His mind was indeed shattered during his vision quest in the spring of 1991. Over the course of what he would refer to as his "explosion" or his "meltdown," Marshall Ledbetter became one of relatively few people to have ever seen "the face of God"[21] in such a manner.

Ledbetter's post titled "Arcadia" provides keen and sobering insights into Ledbetter's experience with Florida psychiatric hospitals and the way society manages what he calls the "unfortunate defectives."[22] Ledbetter goes into considerable detail documenting his time spent at G. Pierce Wood Memorial Hospital in Arcadia. He minces no words: "Nothing justifies Florida's state hospitals. No crime by any single individual, no matter how horrendous, justifies the existence of these death camps."[23] As discussed above, G. Pierce Wood hospital was well known for patient abuse, mistreatment, and assault at the hands of hospital staff. Ledbetter witnessed the horrors of the place before it was finally shut down and would have been there close to the very end. He prefaces his remarks about the hospital by saying:

For those of you unfamiliar with the State of Florida, its government, by and large, is controlled by moneyed white trash, descendants of the original citrus and cattle barons who view political office not as a vehicle for public service, but rather as a trough to feed at, a means by which they can influence zoning regulations, taxes, and pollution laws for the benefit of themselves and their families, in a manner much akin to what one finds in Arabic societies, where humanity never evolved past the family and tribal level. . . . They have no motivation whatsoever to exhibit any type of empathy, or even sympathy, towards unrelated unfortunates. . . . Florida State Hospital, Arcadia, is a hospital in name only. Typically a hospital, by its very definition, is a site designed for healing of the sick. . . . Arcadia is the expression of an altogether different philosophy . . . that views the sick not merely as economic liabilities and embarrassments to polite society, but as a terrifying reminder to every individual outside the hospital grounds that they're only one unpredictable manic episode or head-trauma-inducing automobile accident away from joining the ranks of the living dead in the Haldol Auschwitz, so you'd better sweep them under the rug. It is one of the most terrifying experiences the United States of America has to offer its unfortunates. Severely underfunded and understaffed, with grounds so sprawling the staff can't patrol them and dormitories designed for pilots, not mental patients, anything and everything happens here. Female patients prostitute themselves for cigarettes on the outskirts of the vast, grassy fields that surround the main facility. The more violent patients square off with disposable razors in the communal bathroom while everyone else tries to get the hell out of their way, or go to it with stainless steel forks in the lunchroom. Patients/Inmates are bunked down four to a 10' by 16' room. Fights, rape, extortion, violence, forced medications—all on a daily basis. Arcadia is a living testament to our current society's apparent belief that mental illness is not only a crime, but the greatest crime one could commit, and hence deserving of the greatest punishments.[24]

Ledbetter provides a horrifying, firsthand assessment of the abysmal conditions at this public mental-health facility. His criticisms are remarkably well focused and clearly articulated. His experiences at other psychiatric hospitals had placed him in a unique position to assess their functioning and effectiveness.

Compared to Arcadia, Marshall says, Chattahoochee was "a model of efficiency."[25] Chattahoochee had been "designed and built for the specific purpose of warehousing madmen. Solitary cells. Line-of-sight control of the pod by staffers working the control room. Locks on every single door." Marshall also said that "Chattahoochee attracted a better class of lunatics than Arcadia." There, Ledbetter said, patients "could at least define themselves as 'criminal,' . . . whether it be a car thief, or a pyromaniac." At G. Pierce Wood, on the other hand, he writes, the residents "were . . . full on rejects, Baker Act victims, people not even facing a charge because they were too fucked-up to even figure out how to pull a charge, marking time in Hell."[26]

Ledbetter decried the injustice of a society deciding it is "more humane to warehouse" psychiatric patients "for 50 years in an asylum, cheek-to-jowl with psychotic murderers, fearing for their life every hour of the day, than just mercifully shoot them in the head and be done with it."

He asks his reader: "Does that sound harsh to you? If it does, then volunteer to take them into your home, or have them live next to yours. If you don't want to do that, then have the courage to pick up the gun and pull the trigger yourself. But we're a state of 10 million-plus Pontius Pilates, quite willing to pay the taxes necessary to wash our hands of the matter. The pathos one sees in the eyes of the people there is almost too unbearable to witness. And this is done in the name of the people of the State of Florida, by us, our own. 'Father forgive them; for they not know what they do.'"[27]

In 2001 a federal judge ruled that, despite all the reports, investigations, and litigation, care at G. Pierce Wood Memorial Hospital was nonetheless legally adequate.[28] Yet this decision was not enough to stem the flood of calls to close the institution after even more evidence of injury, abuse, and death came to light. These included a patient who died of hypothermia after being left in a bathtub, someone "who cut off both hands on a table saw," and a twenty-one-year-old man who died with "toxic levels of medication in his body."[29] In February 2002 the State of Florida finally closed the hospital. It was billed as a cost-cutting measure for the government and an example of the move toward community-oriented care for the mentally ill.[30]

Marshall's final post is dated March 21, 2002. It is titled "The Al Aqsa Martyrs' Brigade, or How Israel's Likud Party Is Learning, to Its Great Consternation, the True Price of *Lebensraum*." The rant offered Marshall's perspective on the Israeli/Palestinian conflict. The question of Palestine had been a long-standing interest for Ledbetter. Back in 1996 he had told readers of "Tales of Psychoboy" that "Just when I'd almost lost my faith in humanity, the Palestinians come along to re-instill it. Forced into camps because Israelis need 'lebensraum,' used as virtual slave labor, denied basic human rights, treated as scum by the 'Tribe of David—God's Chosen People,' they are willing to fight and die in the streets for self-determination."[31] Six years later, Marshall noted the irony of Israelis treating Palestinians so cruelly and then asks: "What exactly do any of these suicide bombers have to lose? Do they have any hope for the future?"[32]

About six weeks after Ledbetter made this post, the Winter Haven Police Department got a call to do a welfare check on Marshall Ledbetter. Officers Christopher Bracken and David Clark responded. Marshall informed them that he was "being controlled by Al Qaeda."[33] He stated that "several government agencies are observing him and are out to get him." Ledbetter said "he had left a phone message for Senator [and former Florida governor] Bob Graham." Although Ledbetter had "made no specific threats against Graham," he had told Officer Clark that "he hopes Senator Graham takes his warning seriously."[34] Marshall also said that "if he had to go higher than he did in 1991, then he would." Ledbetter did not elaborate. He did say, however, that "poisoning of water and overthrowing the government were the only way he and his friends can be liberated."[35]

Such behavior caused Marshall to be "Baker Acted" once again. He was first taken to Winter Haven Hospital and then transferred to the Crisis Stabilization Unit at the Peace River Center in Bartow, about twenty minutes south. Peace River is "a locked 30 bed receiving facility for Florida's Baker Act" serving residents of Polk, Highlands, and Hardee Counties. Its mission is to provide "psychiatric stabilization services including individual and group therapy, medication management, and education, discharge planning and referrals, and family education."[36]

FDLE special agent Scott Bovee looked into Ledbetter's file. He learned about Marshall's action at the state capitol almost eleven years earlier. Bovee reported that "Ledbetter had barricaded himself in the Florida Capitol building and told the authorities that he had taken a hostage. After a five-hour standoff, Ledbetter surrendered and no hostage had actually been taken." Bovee consulted with state and federal law enforcement, and also with Senator Graham's staff. The special agent then "produced an updated BOLO [Be On the Look Out] flyer concerning Ledbetter's actions and disseminated it to FDLE, Capitol Police, Senator Graham's staff and the U.S. Capitol Police." Bovee described Ledbetter's occupation of the state capitol in 1991, his threat to terminate the Blue Key Club seven years later, and his more recent interactions with the law. The BOLO flyer closed with the directive that "should Ledbetter be observed at any government events or installations, exercise caution and document his actions."[37]

On May 15, 2002, FDLE special agent William Miles visited Marshall at Peace River. He discovered that Ledbetter was "well known to the Peace River Center and had been a patient many times in the past."[38] Because portions of Ledbetter's official mental-health records have been redacted, we don't know how Ledbetter was diagnosed during his last visit to Peace River in May 2002. We don't know what treatment he received or how his present visit was contextualized relative to his earlier ones. We do know that Marshall's doctor at Peace River, Victoria Quezon, told Special Agent Miles that she had "never seen Ledbetter in a violent state and believed him to be 'harmless.'"[39]

Exit

I've been straying from a worthwhile path. I have allowed my rage to consume my judgment. Rage leads to lack of compassion.

Marshall Ledbetter, "Tales of Psychoboy," October 8, 1996

There is no doubt that healthy-mindedness is inadequate as a philosophical doctrine, because the evil facts which it refuses positively to account for are a genuine portion of reality; and they may after all be the best key to life's significance, and possibly the only openers of our eyes to the deepest levels of truth.

William James, *The Varieties of Religious Experience*

On July 16, 2003, Special Agent Charles Guthrie of the Florida Department of Law Enforcement sent a message to the Mansion Protection Operations Section of his organization. He told them Marshall Ledbetter was dead.

Marshall's body had been discovered by his brother and father around 1:00 a.m. on July 15. Marshall was thirty-four years old. Just a couple of weeks earlier, some friends had helped him move into a new apartment in Winter Haven. He was living by himself and getting used to the new place. One evening he called his mother. Although she had detected a change in her son's behavior since his last visit to the Peace River Center, he seemed to be making progress. From her vantage point, Marshall "seemed calm and resigned to trying to stay grounded." She reflects: "He wanted a night out with me, which was unusual for him. We shared a movie and a late dinner before I drove him back to his

Marshall Ledbetter, age 30.
Photo courtesy of Sharon
Graham.

apartment. . . . I was so proud of how well he seemed to be doing. . . .
I told him he would be just fine." They embraced as she dropped him
off. She didn't realize it at the time, but tragically, "that hug good-night
would be my last hug from Marshall."[1]

On July 14, 2003, Ledbetter left his apartment, returned to his
childhood home, and committed suicide in his old bedroom. He was
wearing blue, knee-length denim shorts, white socks, sneakers, and
a multicolored fish shirt. He had ended it all at about 10:00 p.m. He
had lifted a loaded shotgun to his face, wrapped his mouth around the
around the muzzle, and pulled the trigger. Twenty round lead pellets
rocketed through his skull at 900 miles per hour. Forensic tests proved
negative for drugs and alcohol.

Ledbetter's family and friends were devastated, particularly Arlen
and Marshall Sr., who were the ones to find the body. One can hardly
imagine a more horrible circumstance to befall a father and a brother.

They kept everyone else away. A society whose young commit suicide is not a healthy society. Children are not supposed to die before their parents. Given the preponderance of guns in U.S. society—roughly eighty-nine for every one hundred people[2]—ending one's life with a firearm is, as *New York Times Magazine* contributor Scott Anderson tells us, "the most common method of suicide in the United States."[3] It is also the most lethal. Suicide by shotgun is a particularly gruesome and absolutist gesture, the choice of Ernest Hemingway, Kurt Cobain, and Hunter S. Thompson. The torments of the mind are conquered as the brain is obliterated.

"I can't say I was surprised," says Bradley Pepperman, one of Ledbetter's oldest friends from Landis Hall, after hearing about Marshall's death and the manner in which it occurred. Psychiatrist Kay Jamison reports that "70 to 90 percent of all suicides are associated with manic-depressive or depressive illness; therefore, if an individual has committed suicide, it is almost always the case that a mood disorder was at least contributory."[4] Ledbetter did leave a suicide note, which his mother says was "brief." He "asked for our forgiveness, stated he could no longer live his life this way and closed with saying he loved each and every one of us."[5]

Death by suicide is perplexing to onlookers and demonstrates the real limits of social inquiry. We are taught to try to always understand the motivations and meanings that drive individuals to action, but how does one comprehend the incomprehensible? There is an unavoidable, inherent opacity in understanding suicide, both as casual observer and social researcher, that is impossible to overcome. We know very little about Ledbetter's state of mind at the end of his life and have no idea if he succumbed to suicide's "dark passion"[6] with despair, for example, exhaustion, or as a final act of resistance.

Although it was posted more than a year earlier, one of Ledbetter's final website rants had discussed the subject of mercy killing, of shooting the mentally ill in the head and putting them out of their misery. Perhaps at some level Marshall's words hit too close to home, and he suddenly realized it would be hypocritical to make such a claim on others without having the courage to do so himself. At the end of the day, maybe all that needs to be said is that Marshall felt it was time to take another walk. He was compelled toward a terminally transformative action. Certainly Ledbetter was in the midst of what Scott Anderson calls a "mind tumble," as he had been, on and off, for some time. In a letter to the editor of the *Winter Haven News Chief* six years earlier, Ledbetter had already sounded world-weary. "I write this not to warn you of any coming revolution," he said. "I myself no longer have the heart for the struggle. I see no point. . . . I feel old and tired at 27."[7]

Although the suicidal urge may have been welling up for years inside Ledbetter, the decision to actually pull the trigger was most likely somewhat impulsive. In a study of suicide survivors by the University of Houston, researchers found that about 70 percent of people attempting suicide made the decision to do so less than an hour before, and 25 percent decided just five minutes prior to the attempt.[8] Research also indicates that people who try to kill themselves often regret doing so almost immediately after the attempt. As one specialist put it, "What was immediately apparent was that none of them had truly wanted to die. They had wanted their inner pain to stop; they wanted some measure of relief; and this was the only answer they could find. They were in spiritual agony, and they sought a physical solution."[9]

We have very little information about Marshall's life between his last visit to the Peace River Center in May and June 2002 and when he ended his own life in July 2003. Kyle Bermingham, a former police officer and friend of Marshall's, is one of the few witnesses of Ledbetter's last days. The two had met in 1999, and they got to know each other playing matches of chess at the Office Pub in Winter Haven. Though Bermingham didn't drink alcohol at the time and was slightly less liberal than Marshall, he says he enjoyed having conversations with Ledbetter and debating various topics with him, whether U.S. foreign policy, for example, the legalization of drugs, or the politics of the welfare state. Bermingham remembers Marshall as "a very quick talker. . . . The rebuttal was already there, instantly."[10] Ledbetter would invariably win the chess games, even when he was highly intoxicated. He would "kick my ass all over the chessboard," Bermingham remembers. As they played, Marshall would make editorial comments about the world's great chess players, historic matches, and famous chess strategy. Bermingham says that during his early encounters and interactions with Marshall Ledbetter, there was no indication that his friend had any type of mental illness or impairment.

In early May 2002, Bermingham got a phone call from Marshall. He says Ledbetter would occasionally call him needing a ride somewhere, or asking for a piece of advice. On this occasion, Marshall needed a ride to the Army-Navy store in Winter Haven. Bermingham picked him up and took him to the store. He asked Ledbetter what exactly he wanted. He wouldn't say, but Bermingham sensed that Ledbetter "felt the need to prepare for something."[11] Marshall was not particularly coherent and seemed a little paranoid. Words were coming out of his mouth, but they weren't making sense, like someone talking in his sleep. The two wandered around the store for a few minutes until Bermingham gently told Marshall he probably really didn't need to buy anything at the store that day, and they left.

A few days later, Bermingham says, he got another call from Marshall. His friend needed more help. He was stranded at Lake Howard in Winter Haven. Bermingham drove over to meet him and found that Marshall had a flat tire on his bicycle. He says that Ledbetter seemed a little dirty and disheveled, and again he wasn't making much sense. Marshall seemed worried and very frustrated over his deflated tire. Bermingham says that Marshall "couldn't understand why it wasn't working."[12]

Clearly, Ledbetter was experiencing some sort of a breakdown and was having trouble coping. About three days later he would be committed to the Crisis Stabilization Unit at Peace River Center in Bartow. It would be his final visit. He was in no position to refuse treatment. Bermingham, who says he has dealt with many Baker Act cases over the years in the context of his work as a police officer, says that in his experience most people who are "Baker Acted" and sent to a place like Peace River are released within seventy-two hours. Yet Bermingham says that Marshall was kept at the facility for at least three weeks and possibly for as long as nine weeks.[13]

It appears that Marshall was inside the Peace River facility on June 11, 2002, when he wrote a letter to his daughter. It said: "Dear Livia, I'm a spook. I work under DIA's INSCOM Division doing intel and field operations for the USAF's FAC RAVEN Team. I'm affiliated w/ 'Red Cell,' but do not operate under their command. I'm sorry I haven't been around much lately, but these are desperate times. Signed, 'Greif.'"[14] What is notable about this message is that while all the signifiers are "real," in the sense that they have an existence in the material world, they are also all entirely a product of Ledbetter's imagination. Unless Marshall was under some truly deep cover like the aforementioned George Blake (alluded to in "Tales of Psychoboy"), such outlandish claims can only be accepted as a delusional fantasy.

We don't know what medication Marshall was prescribed at Peace River, but it seems to have been very powerful. If Marshall had been experiencing an acute manic swing, his treatment team would have been trying to bring him down to Earth. Yet whatever drugs Marshall was given during those weeks at Peace River seemed to overwhelm him and took him too far in the opposite direction. Now, suddenly, Ledbetter was in a state of almost total depression and lethargy. The mind-dulling side effects of his treatment were severe, seriously changing his mood, contorting his body, and causing an inability to speak.[15]

One on occasion, Marshall's mother visited her son at Peace River and was troubled to see his jaw jutting out at an odd angle, pushing his head back. She says it was due to the medicine they had given him. She adds that "the jutting out of Marshall's jaw was not permanent." When he "returned home and discontinued use of that medication, the muscle spasms that caused this problem stopped, allowing his body to return to normal."[16]

Kyle Bermingham visited Marshall twice during his last stay at Peace River, once in May and once in June of 2002. On the first visit, he brought his chess set with him, hoping to make Marshall feel better and take his mind off his situation. Bermingham was alarmed at the sight of Ledbetter when his friend was brought into the visitation room. He says Marshall seemed like the stereotypical "schizophrenic shuffling around on medication." Kyle says Ledbetter recognized him but didn't seem very excited about him being there. Bermingham beat him easily at chess. He says Marshall was just moving the pieces around the board and "couldn't think to form a strategy."[17] As he was leaving, Bermingham went to give Marshall a hug. Ledbetter flinched and turned away.

One individual who might have understood what Ledbetter was going through at the Peace River Center would have been Stanley Williams, co-founder of the Los Angeles–based Crips street gang. After a lengthy term on California's death row protesting his innocence for a capital crime he says he did not commit, Williams was put to death in 2005, but not before being nominated for the Nobel Peace Prize for his children's books and efforts to stop gang violence. In 1979, soon after he was arrested on the murder warrant, Williams was held in a Los Angeles detention center known as "High Power." There he was administered powerful psychoactive drugs against his will, often smuggled into his food and beverages. His account of the experience may provide a window into Ledbetter's state of mind in the months before his death. Williams writes: "I had spent purposeless years under the influence of drugs such as PCP and LSD. I will never forget the weird trips I experienced nor the violent aggression I initiated because of my personal drug use. Nevertheless, the psychopharmacology employed against me in [prison] proved far more devastating. It was like being buried alive. I felt my brain was suffocating, felt as if I was falling through space deep into nothingness. This was nothing like getting high off street drugs. The Medical Unit's medication was a mind killer."[18] From what little we know of his days at Peace River, it seems Marshall would have been able to relate well to these sentiments.

Kyle Bermingham was glad to see Marshall back at the Office Pub in Winter Haven in the fall of 2002. Ledbetter seemed to be doing much better than he had been during his stay at Peace River, but Bermingham says there was something noticeably different. Marshall no longer came across as the gregarious, super-smart, overexcited, talkative person he once was. "The Marshall I knew prior to going to Peace River was not the same person when he came out," Bermingham says. Marshall had sadly lost much of his spark. He seemed blunted intellectually. Ledbetter stopped going out socially. He went from drinking and playing chess at the Office Pub regularly twice a week to showing up about once a month. And when he did make an appearance, he didn't drink; he just played chess and went home. Yet in spite of his apparent cognitive decline, Bermingham says, Ledbetter still beat him consistently at chess. He was "far and away the better player."[19]

Conrad Arbaugh, another Winter Haven friend, also says that Marshall changed considerably after his last visit to the Peace River Center. He says that Ledbetter had been a generally lively person before being admitted to the clinic, but this last round of treatment "took the edge off that." Arbaugh says, "To me, that's what hurt him the most, was those meds."[20] Ledbetter had always been not only exceptionally intelligent but also loquacious and funny. He would "talk a mile a minute," Arbaugh says, especially when his favorite topics of sports, politics, and history were involved. But whatever treatment Marshall had received at Peace River slowed him down considerably. "Towards the end," Arbaugh said, "his mouth couldn't keep up." Losing such verbal agility must have been torture for Marshall. "You know he wanted to talk," Arbaugh says. "It was sad."[21]

Marshall's obituary ran in the *Lakeland Ledger* on July 17, 2003. A visitation and a memorial service were held at the Ott-Laughlin Funeral Home on K-Ville Avenue in Auburndale. Ledbetter's body was cremated. The funeral service was packed with friends, family members, and casual acquaintances. Arbaugh says the funeral was standing-room only.[22] There were "so many people, so many cars," Bermingham remembers, "such a diverse crowd."[23] All the regulars from the Office Pub were there to show their respect. People shared stories, memories, and anecdotes about Marshall. Others sent out pleas for people in the audience to get help if they ever found themselves in a similar bind. Jody Keel, the owner of the Office Pub, invited everyone back to the bar after the service for an impromptu wake. Kyle Bermingham took the king piece from his chess set and presented it as a gift to Arlen. A plaque of remembrance in Marshall's name was made and hung on Ott-Laughlin's Memorial Wall. To this day, flowers often appear beneath it.

Making Sense of Marshall Ledbetter

> Companies take our inner aspirations and fears and mold these into a strategy designed to get us to consume drugs more faithfully than we would do if we were living in a totalitarian regime and were ordered to consume.
>
> **David Healy,** *Mania*

> The producers seem to have forgotten that the point of propaganda is to convince, not confuse. Maybe they have their own agenda, though, and are purposefully confusing the audience, operating on the assumption that the viewers will continue watching in a desperate, and ultimately futile, attempt to sort through the confusion said programming has induced.
>
> **Marshall Ledbetter, "03-08-02"**

So, where does this all leave us? Was Marshall Ledbetter just a highly strung, overeducated, yet essentially harmless prankster, too smart for his own good, living in a world that didn't understand him? Did he really have a mental illness? If so, was it congenital, brought on by Ledbetter's own drug use, or caused by the unintended consequences of the diagnosis itself? Did his situation improve or worsen through treatment by the State of Florida's mental-health apparatus?

Although he wasn't always the most helpful client, Marshall clearly did get some of the help he needed at Florida State Hospital in Chattahoochee. The recommendations from Dr. Jill Schwartz upon his release from the hospital in January 1992, however, stressed the need for Ledbetter to tackle his substance abuse and to participate in individual and family counseling. All of this sounds like a good start, but due to the inherently private nature of mental-health treatment we know very little about the extent of follow-up over the next twelve years. Moreover, as a more or less rational social actor with some degree of agency, Ledbetter should not be absolved of all responsibility. One can only heap so much blame on other people and institutions. Ledbetter's "culture jamming" would at times be directed at himself and subvert his own recovery. He was probably not doing himself any favors, for example, by self-medicating with alcohol and other drugs while also taking prescribed psychiatric medicine.

People like Ledbetter who have some sort of history and association with mental illness are becoming a lot more common in society. In a 2011 phone interview, Winter Haven's chief of police, Gary Hester, estimated that most of the daily duties of his eighty-three police officers involve dealing with what he calls the problems of "dysfunctional people." Hester estimates that every day in Winter Haven—a city with a population of about twenty-eight thousand—approximately three people are "Baker Acted" for one reason or another. He also says that the police station regularly gets phone calls from individuals who think their neighbors are watching them, that black helicopters are hovering outside their windows, or that they are being eaten by rats. Before long the dispatchers begin to recognize the repeat callers and prioritize their complaints accordingly, but the calls and follow-ups are logged nonetheless.[1]

Tony Judt's *Ill Fares the Land* speaks to the broader historical and social forces that provide the context for many of the issues discussed in this book. Judt writes that in postindustrial societies in general and in the United States in particular, we are facing "a coming age of uncertainty," especially among young people who cannot find work. He writes that "the growing number of people who will have good reason to feel superfluous to the economic life of their society cannot help but pose a serious social challenge."[2] As a society, what do we do with the people who can't or won't fit in, who have become derailed from the tracks of social life?

Insane asylums have morphed into psychiatric hospitals, which have turned into crisis stabilization units. These are the social spaces of last resort, society's waiting areas for those who can no longer function "on the outside." Crisis stabilization units temporarily envelop patients in a culture of security and health, check vital signs, assess prospects, dispense counseling, prescribe medicine, and then send them on their way. Such organizations (or something like them) are obviously indispensable to and respond to real needs in society, but people can't stay there forever. They are also often quite expensive, creating costs that can weigh heavily on patients and families. Like emergency rooms, crisis stabilization units are not designed for long-term care, but people who need help often end up relying on them when they have no alternative.

From a sociological perspective, the quality and quantity of social networks and relationships (to individuals, groups, and organizations) are essential to understanding problems experienced by individuals in society. What the classical social theorist Émile Durkheim described as "organic solidarity" can only occur if everyone is allowed to play a unique and meaningful role in the division of labor by occupying a position in society on which others come to depend.[3] Yet organic solidarity today is often a chimera, especially for the youth of the working and middle classes, whose chances for social mobility in the new economy are often precarious at best. It is always difficult for young people to find their place in society, but it seems like it is becoming even harder today. The main identity that Marshall Ledbetter embraced in his early twenties was that of a "clown dancer"—not an occupation with favorable long-term career prospects. He expressed an interest—which was met with skepticism by his psychological examiner—in learning more about his Cherokee ancestry, and possibly moving to the North Carolina mountains to live on an Indian reservation. Mainstream American culture doesn't make it easy for young people to have transformative experiences such as these. They are considered anathema to the imperatives of school, work, and family. Especially in times of economic contraction, younger generations of people—many of them males— are left to founder. Too often it seems that highly intelligent, passionate young people begin their lives with such promise, only to burn out well before their time. As Marshall's friend Andrew Arvesen aptly notes, "Our society is hard on really smart young people."[4]

Given the manner in which Ledbetter ended his life, it is tempting to conclude that his mental illness was ultimately the main culprit behind all the troubles he experienced. Perhaps Spence and Kling, the psychologists who diagnosed Marshall as suffering from bipolar disorder back in 1991, were right after all. Certainly there should be no shame in mental illness these days. And as Kay Jamison argues, there is also a noble history of creative people who have suffered from something like manic depression. As an artistically inclined person—writer, photographer, rapper, cartoonist, and so on—it seems plausible that Marshall Ledbetter, like the subjects in Jamison's book, was also "touched with fire."[5]

But there is also ample reason to be critical of the mental-health treatment Ledbetter received. Ledbetter was under some kind of psychiatric care for about twelve years. Research indicates that long-term psychotropic drug use can lead to diminished and permanent changes in neurological functioning. Psychiatric patients today are on "a cocktail of psychoactive drugs prescribed for a cocktail of diagnoses."[6] As Dr. Marcia Angell, senior lecturer in social medicine at Harvard Medical School, writes, the "use of antipsychotic drugs is associated with shrinkage of the brain, and . . . the effect is directly related to the dose and duration of treatment."[7] We can only speculate how much of Marshall Ledbetter's own medical history—especially the rapid cognitive decline a year before his suicide—might be understood in light of research such as this. It may also be the case that during his last visit to the Peace River Center his treatment team simply decided to pull out all the stops, insistent on seeing a tangible change in Ledbetter's behavior and continued until such an outcome was achieved.

As it happened, Marshall would never let Peace River treat him again. He even told this to his mother. As they were driving back to his apartment in Winter Haven after what would be their last meal together, Marshall rather casually made a statement that would foreshadow his death. "Mom, I'm never going back to Peace River," he said to her. His mother interpreted this comment as a positive sign, and took it to mean that Marshall thought he no longer needed hospitalization. She congratulated her son on the progress he had made. But after he died, Marshall's mother realized he had been trying to tell her something else. She did not see it at the time, but Marshall was approaching his metaphorical vanishing point. He could no longer shoulder the burden he was carrying.

Despite the insistence of many researchers on the genetic basis of mental illness, sociologists might ask whether and to what extent Ledbetter's troubles became a kind of self-fulfilling prophecy. As human beings, we are all ultimately conformists. Life is, in many ways, a search for social recognition, and it is difficult not to accept the judgments of those around us, especially when they are in positions of power. Managing the label of mental illness is no easy task.[8] Sociologists Amy Kroska and Sarah Harkness write, "When individuals are diagnosed with a psychiatric disorder, they are placed into a cultural category (e.g. a 'mentally ill person') that . . . damages their material, psychological, and social well-being."[9] Their research indicates that people who are labeled mentally ill are more likely to be demoralized, withdrawn from society, and have fewer job prospects. The ironic fact of going to a psychiatrist (as opposed to any other medical practitioner) is that the act of getting a diagnosis can make matters worse, not better. As Dr. Jerome Wakefield of New York University has put it, once individuals are diagnosed as mentally ill, they "will be seen differently by their own families" and "will see themselves differently" as well.[10]

Psychiatry will always be used as a method of social control.[11] One of the most important functions of sociology is to remind us that society is often just as crazy as the people in it, perhaps more so. Ledbetter would agree: "This is a world of madness. . . . All I am sure of is that this system is beginning to disintegrate at the seams."[12] What Erving Goffman described as "total institutions"—for example, psychiatric hospitals, prisons, and military bootcamps—are so named because of the complete control they exert over the individual. Such institutions—like G. Pierce Wood Memorial Hospital in Arcadia—are also often sites of unimaginable ineptitude, corruption, and abuse. As such they must be constantly monitored and scrutinized. We cannot just leave it all to the people in white coats. We cannot turn away and wash our hands of our responsibility for the people Ledbetter describes as the "unfortunate defectives." It is wrongheaded and cruel for the strident voices who decry the role of the state in society to limit their critique to issues of taxation and regulation and refuse to acknowledge, let alone try to reform, the bureaucratic horrors not only of the U.S. mental-health-care system but the criminal justice system and the immigration system, as well.

At the end of the day, we are forced to conclude that whatever treatment methods were put in to place to try to rehabilitate Marshall Ledbetter simply did not work. The much-vaunted "medical model" failed to produce a healthy outcome. It may be true that if left untreated manic depression can lead, as the psychiatrist Kay Jamison says, to "a worsening of the illness over time."[13] But the irony of our tale is that Marshall *was* treated, and treated quite extensively, by a number of highly qualified, state-certified mental-health professionals over and over again for many years. Suicide was still the result. As Scott Anderson writes, despite "whole new generations of antidepressant drugs that have been developed," today "the nation's suicide rate is almost precisely what it was in 1965."[14] If the pharmaceutical approach to treating conditions like bipolar disorder is working so well, we would expect the statistics to reflect it. The fact that we don't see any difference indicates that as a society we might want to be looking at alternatives to the way we manage the mentally ill.

In his heyday, Marshall Ledbetter identified as a kind of punk rock and rap music listening, culture-jamming anarchist. He belonged to a subculture in which some forms of proscribed drug use were relatively normalized. Ledbetter enjoyed the experiences that psychedelic drugs and marijuana, in particular, afforded him. In doing so, he adhered to what can be called a "libertarian" perspective on intoxicants, one that objects on principle to the state dictating the types of substances people can put in their bodies. There is a clear resemblance between this worldview and the one espoused by the "Freak Power" movement of the 1970s and its symbolic leader Hunter S. Thompson.

One can easily imagine someone like Thompson understanding in a deep and vital way the real meaning behind Marshall Ledbetter's occupation of the Florida capitol back in June 1991. The gonzo journalist might have gotten a kick out of Ledbetter's writings and disagreed with missives like this one only in the details: "Mr. Responsible Citizen, you suck. You've got a species level extinction event happening under your nose and you're worried about keeping me away from some mushrooms. Get a life. . . . I don't go to city commission meetings griping about these junkie Christians who keep communing in church every Sunday, getting a feedback loop pheromone fix from being in a room with a few hundred other sweating monkeys. . . . Why did you allow, or worse, encourage Authority to ban all other sacraments?"[15]

Yet Hunter S. Thompson was never prosecuted for his shenanigans or drug use, mainly because he could afford to pay for his privacy. It is apparently one thing to be a best-selling author and countercultural icon living in Woody Creek, Colorado, and another to be a homeless college student in North Florida trying to gain a foothold on reality. Excesses among the celebrity elite are more easily forgiven.

As another contrasting case, take the spectacular fall from grace of cultural icon Charlie Sheen. The popular television actor had what was obviously something close to a nasty nervous breakdown in 2011. Disturbing allegations about drugs, alcohol, pornographic film stars, trips to the Bahamas, and domestic violence were broadcast around the world. Yet remarkably, media accounts never suggested the actor's behavior might be pathological—his antics were framed simply as just another film star behaving badly. Unlike Ledbetter, Sheen had the money and resources to avoid having the subject of mental illness brought into the conversation, let alone morphing into a label that became stuck to his identity. His status allowed him to forge a different path. The takeaway message appears to be that if you have the wealth and the social capital, it is perfectly acceptable to go around proclaiming yourself to be a "warlock from Mars," bragging about the $250,000 worth of cocaine in your suitcase and your sex life with a stable of "goddesses." Lacking such privilege and social importance on the other hand, you risk being committed to a psychiatric hospital or similar sort of facility.

Obviously, Florida (even in the more liberal Tallahassee) is considerably less hedonistic and tolerant than other locales, such as Sheen's Hollywood or Thompson's Aspen. Most likely Ledbetter's more or less unapologetic drug use did not help his case much in the eyes of the law and served as another measure of his mental deficiencies. Such a prohibitionist interpretation, however, refuses to acknowledge the benefits of some mind-altering substances. For example, some psychiatrists now think moderate marijuana usage can be an effective treatment for bipolar affective disorder (BAD), the very illness from which Ledbetter was thought to be suffering.

As C. H. Ashton et al. report: "BAD is often poorly controlled by existing drugs and often involves a polypharmacological medley, including lithium, anticonvulsants, antidepressants, antipsychotics and benzodiazepines. . . . There are good pharmacological reasons for believing that the prescription of synthetic cannabinoids or standardized plant extracts may have a therapeutic potential."[16] Yet Ledbetter's use of marijuana was negatively sanctioned by his mental-health team and considered a hindrance to his therapy instead of being explored as a possible (if only partial) solution to his problems.

While the benefits of medical marijuana are becoming better known, intriguing research is also being conducted on the mental-health benefits of more powerful psychedelic compounds. As noted in work published by the American Medical Association, "the medical value of hallucinogens is again being examined in formal psychiatric settings."[17] One interesting area of study has been on the effects of psilocybin use in terminally ill cancer patients. Researchers have found that patients who were prescribed psilocybin approached the end of their lives with less anxiety, depression, and stress. Investigators suggest that psilocybin may provide a kind of "ontological security" for some patients.[18] Given Marshall Ledbetter's experience with psychedelic mushrooms, it is possible he experienced a similar kind of philosophical comfort even as ended his own life.

Interestingly, the use of psychedelic compounds to treat mental disorders was discovered by Ledbetter one day as he investigated the chemistry behind the prescribed drugs he was taking. As he started to analyze the compounds in his medicine, suddenly everything made sense. Marshall described the attendant epiphany in religious terms: "JESUS CHRIST! ATROPINE! $C_{17}H_{23}NO_3$. I *KNEW* IT! I *KNEW* there was something about that Cogentin that made me feel like I was tripping! Atropine! A belladonna alkaloid! Often used by ladies in the courts of Italy during the middle ages to dilate their eyes—this proving useful in their attempts to feign sexual interest (eye dilation=interest) in courtiers, thus aiding them in court intrigues. Derived from the

deadly nightshade, it is also hallucinogenic. . . . GOD, I NEVER CEASE
TO BE AMAZED AT MY UTTER STUPIDITY. WHY WAS I BITCHING ABOUT
MY MEDS?" Ledbetter explained the cosmic irony: "In '91, indole alkaloid compounds (found in psilocybin mushrooms) provide the inspiration, like Raskolnikov, to commit an offense, and the State of
Florida responds with a course of action that ensures that I will en-
counter Cogentin in '96, a legal, lifetime, pharmaceutical grade belladonna alkaloid hallucinogen! Indeed, I now ingest it with everyone's
nodding approval! THERE IS A GOD AND HIS NAME IS 'MERCY AND
UTTERLY SUBLIME HUMOR'![19] Thank you, Krsna or Yahweh or Who-
ever! . . . Thank you Great Spirit! You have amply rewarded your brave
little warrior! Who cares if I never get to bang Paula Abdul! Cogentin's
better! 1991 was worth it, after all!"[20]

In reflecting on the Ledbetter story, it is impossible not to speculate on what would happen if someone were to break into and occupy
the Florida Capitol Building in a similar manner today. Although some
might agree with the *Tallahassee Democrat*'s Mark Hinson, who writes
that "If some poor kid pulled a Ledbetter on Florida's 22-story Tower
of Power here in the post-Sept. 11 world, we'd probably still be scrub-
bing parts of him off the giant cow mural in the Capitol's lobby,"[21] Leon
County sheriff Larry Campbell thinks the outcome would be the same
as it had been with Ledbetter.

Campbell says his officers regularly deal with "people three bricks
short of a load."[22] Often, he says, such individuals lock themselves inside buildings, and it is job of the police to get them out. Campbell
and his team are always careful interacting with what he calls "squirrels"—people thought to be mentally incapacitated. "You don't want
to hurt someone who is off their rocker," Campbell says. Certainly it is
a testament to Campbell's leadership as a commander, the skills of his
negotiator, and the cooperation of all the different agencies involved
that Ledbetter's standoff with the police ended with no one getting
hurt.

Having spent considerable time researching and thinking about
Ledbetter, my view is that he may be admired in some ways and pitied in others. Even if one doesn't find the overall arc of his biography completely compelling, it is hard to deny Marshall's tremendous

strength of will. People in total institutions like psychiatric hospitals often break down very quickly because they don't have their normal routines, role sets, and relational structures to draw upon. It takes extraordinary resistance for an individual to withstand the demands of imposing authority figures and to courageously say no to their directives. It is also not every day that you hear about people escaping from psychiatric hospitals by clambering over razor wire, but that is exactly what Ledbetter did.

Viewed in political terms, Ledbetter's break-in at the capitol at first seems like an abysmal failure. The CNN broadcast had been faked, so Marshall's demands were never delivered to his would-be followers on the world stage. Marshall also missed a crucial opportunity to explain his motivations to the press as he was being escorted out of the capitol en route to the waiting squad car. Paradoxically, police negotiator Gilda Strickland did a much better job articulating the reasons behind Marshall's occupation of the capitol than Ledbetter did himself.[23] Ledbetter's protest did indeed go "viral" for a couple of news cycles, but it became muted once he was institutionalized.

Yet despite its apparent meaninglessness, Ledbetter's storming of the capitol did feed into small currents of resistance in Tallahassee that have fueled waves of student protest ever since. Former *Florida Flambeau* editor Ron Matus, for example, says that contrary to Ledbetter's assessment, students at Florida State did become more radicalized after his action at the capitol. A former reporter for the *Tampa Bay Times* and now an educational policy expert in Florida, Matus calls the Ledbetter incident a "seminal event." He says it was "a crazy, wacky, idealistic bit of theater . . . protest theater."[24]

"At the time," Matus comments, "it was an inspiring event to many of us."[25] He quickly adds: "Not that we condoned what he did—he could have gotten himself and/or others hurt, he destroyed property, he wasted a lot of people's time. In that sense, it was NOT cool, then, or now." Yet Matus also states that "Ledbetter's crazy takeover created an atmosphere of activism, possibility and hope." Matus took Marshall's main message to be "Make shit happen," and he says that Marshall himself "made it happen in a big, bold, we-still-talk-about-it-today way."[26]

Matus admits to having been inspired by Ledbetter when he created a new student government group on FSU campus in 1994 called the Progressive Independent Party (PIP). "The Marshall incident wasn't the only thing floating around in the zeitgeist," Matus says. "There was also the *Flambeau's* rich history, FSU's Berkeley of the South moniker; the oh-so-inspiring everything about the Monarchy Party; the Chinese guy who stood in front of the tank; the fall of the Berlin Wall; the House of KAO$; etc." But Matus argues that "Ledbetter was the most compelling example in our backyard. He was one of us." Matus says Marshall pushed "the limits of what we think is possible."[27]

Josh Mitchell, the *Flambeau*[28] reporter who covered the Ledbetter case extensively, suggests that Marshall "was a young student trying to make a statement and that takes a lot of guts."[29] Andrew Arvesen still remembers Ledbetter's "brilliant rants." They were "so clever . . . you could feel the heat of the anger." He says Marshall was "constantly critiquing," using "brilliant parody and mockery. The vein of outrage was always clear."[30] Jonathan Lammers argues that "Marshall's scathing critiques illustrate his acute perceptive abilities and why he could be such an interesting friend."[31]

As we conclude our exploration of Ledbetter, it seems appropriate to include a few examples of his ruthless criticism:

Of the band Hootie and the Blowfish, Ledbetter said: "I actually believe they're a cult out of some university in South Carolina who decided to castrate themselves and then serve up the musical equivalent of Gerber baby-food."[32]

On society: "Coffeeshop equals suckhead bourgeois loudly coughing when I fire up a smoke. Bars equal alcohol-sodden lost souls. Home equals brutal TV vixens."[33]

About media control: "Veteran's Day. Paean to the Nation/State. Tonight . . . Monday Night Football rolls out of Circus Maximus. Lions vs. Chargers. One squad leader/quarterback vs the other, interspersed with Anheuser-Busch and US Army Commercials. Thus the plebeians are nourished and eventually harvested."[34]

On the economy: "Nothing burns me more than these small-town Republicans hypocritically preaching the virtues of economic liberty, whilst their brethren in Congress enact loopholes in the Federal tax

On The Road

I was out drinking with Autobahn the other day. He was originally born in Nazi Germany – Hitler's tarmac brainchild – but Eisenhower was taken with him and invited him over to our country (like any good vampire he couldn't show up without being asked to "step on in." None of us really like him, since, being a Nazi artifact, he's no better for one than a syringe full of heroin and HIV virii (but he must be better than junk because his addiction rate is higher......how many people do you know that have stopped abusing Autobahn once they got a car?), but, like any partner in an abusive relationship, he's convinced us that we can't survive without him (one time when we were drinking together he told me that supermarkets wouldn't exist without him, and that we'd all starve without tractor-trailers hauling food hundreds of miles to us, and I said, "Well, what about the farmer's market," and he said, "That's not air-conditioned!"(Shut me up damn quick)), plus he always buys, so we put up with him. Anyway, we were all getting ripped, I was shooting pool, and he's proceeding to start some shit with some guy at the bar (I can't watch him every second – am I my Autobahn's keeper?), the guy has the temerity to ask him who in the hell did he think he was, and Autobahn went off, "I'M YOUR ASPHALT GOD! YOUR ZONING LAWS, CITIES, SUBURBS, AND "WAY OF LIFE" ARE DESIGNED AROUND MY DOT FUNDED, EVER-GROWING GRID! 20% OF YOUR INCOME GOES TO "TRANSPORTATION COSTS" TO SERVE ME! YOUR OIL, AUTOMOTIVE, AND INSURANCE COMPANIES EXIST TO SERVE ME! YOU SERVE ME THE BLOOD SACRIFICES I DEMAND EVERY DAY, AND CALL THEM "ACCIDENT VICTIMS"! I'M MORE VALUABLE TO YOU THAN YOUR ECOSYSTEM! YOUR NEIGHBOR! YOUR FAMILY! YOUR HUSBAND! YOUR WIFE! YOUR CHILD! I COULD CLAIM ALL OF THEM AND YOU STILL WOULDN'T DISMANTLE ME! I COULD CLAIM YOU TOMORROW, AND NOT A SINGLE PERSON YOU KNOW WOULD BE UPSET ENOUGH TO EVN TRY AND RIP UP SOME OF MY PAVEMENT! THEY WOULD THINK OF YOUR DEATH AS "FATE", OR "SOME DRUNKEN DRIVER'S FAULT, OR A LESSON ON WHY "DRIVING ON TOO LITTLE SLEEP IS DANGEROUS", RATHER THAN THINK ABOUT ME! I HARNESS YOUR GOVERNMENT TO MAKE ME LARGER EVERY DAY! I'M THE BIGGEST SINGLE STRUCTURE IN THE WORLD! I'M RIGHT OUTSIDE YOUR FRONT DOOR! YOU KNOW WHERE TO FIND ME, MOTHERFUCKER!"

Anyway, we finally hustled him out of the bar and into the car before he got punched out. Then we had to use him to get home.

MRLJr 9-19-01

Marshall Ledbetter posted this short story, "On the Road," on his website on September 19, 2001.

law and exemptions that allow multinationals and scum like Samuel Walton's corporation to destroy small businesses nationwide."[35]

With Ledbetter dead, we are missing a critical and singular perspective. My research on this project began with the intention of finding out what happened to the young man who occupied the Florida State Capitol Building in 1991. In the course of my investigations I have come to realize that Ledbetter was as much a writer as he was an activist. In "Tales of Psychoboy" Marshall shares his excitement about getting a short story published in a local literary magazine.[36] Through such writing, as well as occasional letters to the editor, and his website postings, it is clear that Ledbetter wanted to have a positive impact on society.[37] As he wrote to his friends, "Hopefully at least one person prowling around Orlando staring nihilism in the face will be inspired to punch through to the next level. Maybe I will get some feedback from the readers."[38]

Certainly there will be many individuals who will, for whatever reason, dislike or disagree with Ledbetter or simply not appreciate what he had to say. At times Marshall could be obnoxious, frustrating, and hard to handle. But his voice resonated with many people over the course of his relatively short life. Far from being a lunatic, Ledbetter exhibits many characteristics of what Nicholas Murray describes in his biography of Aldous Huxley as a "liberal humanist thinker" who defends "the freedom of the sentient individual" against "bullying by the State, propaganda, conditioning by advertising and marketing, and brainwashing."[39]

The fact that Marshall took his own life demonstrates that, despite his courage, he was also a fragile human being. There is an unavoidable darkness to Marshall's story that cannot be wished away. Ron Matus concedes that "it is hard to look back on the incident so fondly knowing he had these issues which overcame him."[40] Cultural observer Steve MacQueen agrees. He says the story of Ledbetter's capitol takeover "plays like a comedy" but is actually a "lonelier, sadder thing." MacQueen admits to having been "nearly obsessed" and "really intrigued by the story" at the time it happened. To him it looked—as it did to Matus—like Marshall was trying to "tweak the man." MacQueen thought Ledbetter "was in control of the situation," and he wanted him to be a hero. Two decades later, MacQueen doubts whether Marshall was ever in control that morning at the capitol. "I don't feel that way anymore," he says. "Marshall just wasn't making an incredible amount of sense."[41]

Marshall Ledbetter was a very young man, just twenty-two years of age, when he broke into the capitol. His life would never be the same. He died twelve years later, at thirty-four. As may be seen in the story chronicled in this book, Ledbetter made significant contributions to the world over the course of his life, but clearly he was capable of much more. Marshall may be pitied for the wasted potential of his life, the suffering he endured, and that he died in such a violent way. If one accepts the diagnoses of the mental-health experts who suggest that bipolar disorder is primarily genetic, then perhaps much of this was beyond his control. Whatever the ultimate causes, let us conclude now with Mark Hinson, who says it is "hard not to get a kick out of Ledbetter's gloriously misguided attempt to take over Florida one fine June morn."[42]

Acknowledgments

Many individuals helped with this project in various ways. I would first of all like to thank the following people who were kind enough to grant me interviews (either in person, over the phone, or via e-mail): Andrew Arvesen, Jello Biafra, Kyle Bermingham, Chris Boose, Alicia Calandra, Larry Campbell, Gregory Cohen, Ruby Dennis, Jeff Fuller, Julie Fuqua, Sharon Graham, John Griffin, Gary Hester, Mark Hinson, Jonathan Lammers, Livia Ledbetter, Jesse Lovett, Steve MacQueen, Ron Matus, Josh Mitchell, Tracy Morse, Randy Murrell, Wayne Todd, Walter Tschinkel, Mike Vasilinda, and Eric Witherspoon.

I would also like to thank eight additional individuals who agreed to participate in this project but who did so on condition of anonymity. To protect their identity, these people have been given pseudonyms (listed as they appear throughout the book).

I would like to thank the Mountain Goats for allowing me to reproduce the lyrics to "Have to Explode" that appear at the beginning of chapter 3. Lyrics to Townes Van Zandt's song "Sanitarium Blues" that appear at the beginning of chapter 14 are used by permission of Jeanene Van Zandt.

The following friends, colleagues, and family members were a source of encouragement while working on this book: Esther and Taylor Abel, Zubair Amir, Grant Balfour, Bob Barrett, Jon Bassett, Julia Berkowitz, David Brain, Roy Carr, Jason Coleman, Bob Cronin, Harry Dahms, Gwen Davies, Jen Dornan-Fish, Gary Alan Fine, Patricia Fingeroff,

Mike Frederick, Charlie Geer, Mike Glantz, Chad Goldberg, Harry Gould, Joe Grabowski, Rosa Greenbaum, Doug Grider, Harry Hanbury, Mike and Jenny Harrison, Jon Holloway, Larry Isaac, Allen Joseph, Nate Kimble, Robin Kirkpatrick, Paul Kooistra, Doug Locklin, David Mash, Jason Metter, Ed Moore, Steve O'Neill, Bill Poston, Branko Reiger, Buck Rogers, John Romanski, David Sawh, Mellini Sloane, Robert Smith, Rich Templin, Tina Terrill, Lee Vartanian, Rob Watkins, Anne Weaver, and Kevin Witherspoon.

I would like to thank John Wells and Jonathan Lammers for answering many questions and providing many insights. At Lander University, Ben Hawthorne provided key technical support while Adam Haigh and Lisa Wieke were very helpful in locating hard-to-find articles and books. Principal John Hill of Auburndale High School was gracious to let me flip through old yearbooks in his office. I would also like to thank Gina Bevino, director of the Capitol Police; Mary Whittington of the Leon County Courthouse; the Leon County Sheriff's Office; and finally, the staff of the *FSView*, who not only allowed me access to the *Florida Flambeau* archive room but also let me use their photocopier.

Matt Davidson and Garreth Piekarski provided keen criticism on early drafts. Martin Dyckman, Craig Pittman, and an anonymous reviewer offered excellent comments, asked the right questions, and provided productive suggestions for improving the manuscript. Lucy Harrison provided helpful advice about how to begin the story and was kind enough to review the penultimate draft. Larry Hazelrigg gave the final nudge to get the manuscript out the door. I am grateful to Sian Hunter and the University Press of Florida for taking an early interest in the story and helping to transform a fairly rough manuscript into the finished book in front of you. Marthe Walters helped steer the project through its final stages. Copy editor Jonathan Lawrence did a fantastic job polishing up the manuscript and offered excellent suggestions for making the book more readable.

Many thanks to Jason Flom for the excellent photographs he took for this project. I am also very much obliged to Sharon Graham for allowing me to use the family pictures of Marshall Ledbetter that appear in the book.

I am grateful to Joseph Caffentzis for his help formatting Blake Fleetwood's photograph of the Columbia University sit-in and for his help with other illustrations that will appear on this book's website.

A tremendous amount of love and appreciation goes out to my wife, Rebecca Salter Harrison, and my daughters, Liliana and Mirabel, for putting up with me while I was "Ledbettering" (as it came to be called) and giving me the time and space needed to write this book.

The dedication expresses my appreciation to my teachers, those brave individuals who, from elementary to graduate school and beyond, taught me much of what I know about the world. Despite all the challenges facing contemporary education, it deserves remembering that the young will always need mentors.

Notes

Chapter 1. Intruder at the Capitol

1. Dennis interview.
2. Ibid.
3. Lovett interview.
4. Dennis interview.

Chapter 2. A Florida State Awakening

1. With the exception of Carla Savage, Marshall's younger sister, Ledbetter's siblings did not respond to my requests for interviews. I briefly met Marshall Ledbetter Sr. as he was opening up Marshall's Camera in April 2011, but he respectfully declined to comment. Marshall's mother, Sharon Ledbetter (now Sharon Graham), did contact me as the book was being readied for publication, and her kind input is noted throughout the text.
2. This is a pseudonym.
3. Krawchuk interview.
4. Judd, "Eight Hour Siege Ends," 8A.
5. Mitchell, "666 Jelly Doughnuts?" 6.
6. Judd, "Eight Hour Siege Ends," 8A.
7. Kling, "Psychological Report."
8. Graham interview.
9. "Tallahassee," Florida Center for Instructional Technology, http://fcit.usf.edu.
10. MacQueen quoted in Hallenbeck, "New Artistic Director," 3.
11. Roberts, "Tallahassee," 1.
12. Ibid.

13. Jackson's legacy is a controversial one, especially in Tallahassee, where many residents know him primarily for his battles against Native Americans. For years, groups have protested the annual Springtime Tallahassee Parade because it is led by a white member of Tallahassee society dressed as Jackson.

14. Morrison attended FSU for two years before heading out to California and forming the Doors. He was known as something of a prankster. On Saturday, September 28, 1963, following an FSU football game against Texas Christian University which the Seminoles lost 13–0, a drunken Morrison took a police umbrella and helmet out of an open squad car and refused to return them. The act earned him a trip to the Leon County jail on the charge of disturbing the peace and resulted in the infamous mug shot Tallahassee residents cherish.

15. I remember walking along Tennessee Street (aka "the Strip") one evening in the late 1990s. A homeless man asked a group of fraternity brothers for spare change. One of them stopped for a moment, took out his wallet, looked inside, and then flatly responded, "Sorry, all I have is a hundred."

16. For a critical perspective on college culture, one that might easily be applied to FSU, see the song "Terminal Preppie" by *Dead Kennedys*, which includes the following lines: "My ambition in life is to look good on paper / All I want is a slot in some big corporation."

17. Graham interview.

18. This is a pseudonym.

19. Mitchell, "666 Jelly Doughnuts?"

20. Some books by these writers that particularly impressed Marshall include *Jailbird* and *Slaughterhouse Five* by Kurt Vonnegut, *"Surely You're Joking Mr. Feynman!"* by Richard Feynman, and *A Scanner Darkly, The Divine Invasion,* and *The Transmigration of Timothy Archer* by Philip K. Dick.

21. Boehmke interview.

22. This is an psuedonym.

23. Mahler interview.

24. Arvesen interview.

25. Jonathan Lammers, e-mail to author, May 7, 2013.

26. Witherspoon interview.

27. Krawchuk interview.

28. Arvesen interview.

29. This is a pseudonym.

30. Peppe interview.

31. Mahler interview.

32. Krawchuk interview.

33. Boehmke interview.

34. Ibid.

35. Ibid.

36. Mahler interview.

37. Mitchell, "666 Jelly Doughnuts?" Some readers might find it odd that Ledbetter could have become a substitute teacher without a college degree in Polk County in the late 1980s. In fact, it is still possible today. At the time of writing (April 2014) the official website for the Polk County School System states that one can be a substitute teacher in Polk County if one is at least eighteen years old, has a high school diploma, and has at least thirty hours of college credit from an accredited institution.

Chapter 3. The Monarchy Days

1. Mitchell, "666 Jelly Doughnuts?" 6.

2. Tschinkel interview.

3. Tschinkel, e-mail to author, October 25, 2010.

4. Tschinkel interview.

5. Peppe interview. Bert Peppe is a pseudonym.

6. Kling, "Psychological Report," 3.

7. Ibid.

8. Peppe interview.

9. Marshall Ledbetter, "Tales of Psychoboy," September 28, 1996.

10. Griffin interview.

11. Mitchell, "666 Jelly Doughnuts?"

12. Mahler interview.

13. Newberger, *Paula Abdul*, 39. In 2002, Abdul got a second blast of fame as a judge on the reality music talent show *American Idol*.

14. In November 2012 the *Huffington Post* called Skat and Abdul's dance routine "one of the most fondly remembered vignettes from the music video era."

15. Jonathan Lammers, e-mail to author, May 7, 2013.

16. Boose interview.

17. Bennett, *Zuni Fetishes*, 125.

18. Cohen interview.

19. Jonathan Lammers, e-mail to author, May 7, 2013.

20. Ron Matus, e-mail to author, March 25, 2014.

21. "Pamphlet #1, Pg. 14," The Church of the SubGenius, http://www.subgenius.com/pam1/pamphlet_p14.html.

22. Mitchell, "666 Jelly Doughnuts?"

23. Ravenhurst, *Principia Discordia*.

24. Gorightly, *The Prankster and the Conspiracy*, 61.

25. Arvesen interview.

26. Jonathan Lammers, e-mail to author, May 7, 2013.

27. Arvesen interview.

28. Ibid.

29. MacQueen interview.

30. Ibid.

31. "Monarchy Party," http://en.wikipedia.org/wiki/Monarchy_Party.

32. Wells, "The Monarchical Dialectic," 1.

33. Thompson, "Freak Power in the Rockies," 33.

34. Cohen interview.

35. Arvesen interview.

Chapter 4. Vision Quest

1. Mitchell, "666 Jelly Doughnuts?"

2. Ibid.

3. This is a pseudonym.

4. Deon Gondron, e-mail to author, June 10, 2012. Deon Gondron is a pseudonym.

5. See Tymoczko, "The Nitrous Oxide Philosopher."

6. See Campbell, *The Power of Myth*.

7. Chaudhuri and Chaudhuri, *Sacred Path*, 93.

8. Ibid.

9. Leary, *Flashbacks,* 29. For some provocative arguments about psilocybin mushrooms in the context of human evolution, philosophy, and religion, see McKenna, *Food of the Gods*.

10. Leary, *Flashbacks*, 29.

11. Wasson, "Seeking the Magic Mushroom."

12. Leary, *Flashbacks*, 32.

13. Ibid., 55.

14. Ibid.

15. Grob et al., "Pilot Study of Psilocybin Treatment," 72.

16. McKenna, *Food of the Gods*, 7.

17. Quoted in Marks, "Sixties Hero," 36.

18. It is not just American youth who have experimented with the mysterious psilocybe. For an entertaining account from England—one which also addresses the antics of a rebellious college student searching for meaning—see Newell, *Wild Man of Wivenhoe*.

19. Sexton, "Looking for an Organic High?" 16.

20. Ibid., 17.

21. Campbell interview.

22. Riley and Blackman, "Between Prohibitions," 56.

23. McKenna, *Food of the Gods*, 26.

24. Ibid., 249.

25. Griffiths et al., "Psilocybin Occasioned Mystical Experiences"; MacLean, Johnson, and Griffiths, "Mystical Experiences."

26. Grob et al., "Pilot Study of Psilocybin Treatment," 71–78.

27. Riley and Blackman, "Between Prohibitions," 56.

28. Hensley, "Study Finds No Link."

29. Pudlow, "Resistance to Treatment," 1.

30. McKenna, *Food of the Gods*, 51, 32.

31. Kilmister, *White Line Fever*, 59.

32. Ibid.

33. Boehmke interview.

Chapter 5. Iron Horse Adventures

1. Arvesen interview.

2. Graham interview.

3. Sharon Graham says that they contacted this facility after being told that a cheaper facility that charged only $2,500 per week had no space and would have to put Marshall on a waiting list. E-mail to author, April 13, 2014.

4. Graham interview.

5. Peppe interview.

6. Pepperman interview. Bradley Pepperman is a pseudonym.

7. Jonathan Lammers, e-mail to author, May 7, 2013.

8. Ibid.

9. Witherspoon interview.

10. Cohen interview.

11. Ledbetter had probably lifted the plate from his grandfather's Mercedes repair shop in Tampa, where he had worked briefly that spring.

12. Tallahassee Police Department Vehicle/Property Receipt, Case No. 91-23522.

13. Krawchuk interview.

14. Cohen interview.

15. Griffin interview.

16. Van Gieson and Yeomans, "Intruder Disrupts Capitol," 1.

17. Vasilinda, "Capitol Showdown," 3.

18. Cohen interview.

19. Jonathan Lammers, e-mail to author, May 7, 2013.

20. Bradley Pepperman, e-mail to author, March 23, 2012.

21. Krawchuk interview.

22. Peppe interview.

23. Arvesen interview.

24. Witherspoon interview.

25. Mitchell, "666 Jelly Doughnuts?" 7.

26. Boose interview.

27. Thompson, "Freak Power in the Rockies," 34.

28. Lindee Morgan, e-mail to author, April 5, 2014.

29. Peppe interview.

30. I thank Walter Tschinkel for providing a copy of this clip.

31. Quoted in C. Anderson, "They Rapped," 1B.

Chapter 6. A Late Night at the Hogly

1. "Monarchy Party," http://en.wikipedia.org/wiki/Monarchy_Party.

2. Peppe interview.

3. Ibid.

4. Cohen interview.

5. Spence, "Court-Ordered Psycholgical Evaluation," July 2, 1991, 4.

6. Boose interview.

7. Griffin interview.

8. John Griffin, e-mail to author, April 23, 2013.

9. Van Gieson and Yeomans, "Intruder Disrupts Capitol," 2.

Chapter 7. Capitol Showdown

1. Miller, *Capitol*, 9.

2. "Symbols," Florida Department of State, accessed September 1, 2013, http://www.flheritage.com/facts/symbols/seals.cfm.

3. Roberts, "Tallahassee," 1.

4. Miller, *Capitol*, 45.

5. Sexton, "Guide to the Capitol."

6. Bruns, "Weak Link."

7. Ibid.

8. Miller, *Capitol*, 40–41.

9. Hallifax, "Man Surrenders."

10. United Press International, "Man Who Barricaded Himself in Capitol."

11. Todd interview.

12. Cotterell, "Senate Sergeant-at-Arms Retires," 1.

13. Todd interview.

14. Fuqua interview.

Chapter 8. The State Responds

1. Todd interview.

2. Cotterell, "Senate Sergeant-at-Arms Retires."

3. Pretti, "Roast the Leon County Sheriff."

4. Waters, "Campbell in Renewed Fight."

5. Campbell interview.

6. Hallifax, "Man Barricades Self."

7. Sutton, "Student Holds Up Capitol," 1B.

8. Van Gieson and Yeomans, "Intruder Disrupts Capitol."

9. Campbell interview.

10. The author's attempts to locate Strickland to comment on the case were unsuccessful.

11. Steven Profit declined to be interviewed for this book.

12. Campbell interview.

13. Ibid.

14. Mike Vasilinda, e-mail to author, April 22, 2013.

15. Vasilinda interview.

16. Vasilinda, "Raw Footage."

17. Ibid.

18. Ibid.

19. Bomb technician Jesse Lovett had been called in to investigate this object at about 6:00 a.m. It had not taken him long to determine that it was a liquor bottle and not a bomb. Lovett interview.

20. Vasilinda, "Raw Footage."

21. Peppe interview.

22. Sutton, "Student Holds Up Capitol."

23. Lovett interview.

24. Jeff Fuller, e-mail to author, September 3, 2013.

25. Lovett interview.

26. Campbell interview. Jeff Fuller, former agent with the South Carolina Law Enforcement Division, says that when he picked up the Hornet in Tallahassee in 1998 it was not operational. It was dismantled and used for parts on other machines.

27. Vasilinda, "Raw Footage."

28. Ibid.

29. Vasilinda, "Raw Footage."

30. Ibid.

31. Mike Vasilinda, e-mail to author, April 22, 2013.

32. Ibid.

33. Campbell interview.

Chapter 9. Aftermath

1. Campbell interview.

2. United Press International, "Man Who Barricaded Himself in Capitol," 1.

3. Cotterell, "Senate Sergeant-at-Arms," 1.

4. Ibid., 2.

5. Ibid.

6. Ibid., 3.

7. Campbell interview.

8. Todd interview.

9. Fuqua interview.

10. Hallifax "Man Surrenders."

11. Vasilinda, "Raw Footage."

12. Ibid.

13. Ibid.

14. Ibid.

15. Kastner, "Leary's in Town."

16. Vasilinda, "Raw Footage."

17. Ibid.

18. Ibid.

19. Ibid.

20. Ibid.

21. Van Gieson and Yeomans, "Intruder Disrupts Capitol," 2.

22. Hallifax, "Man Surrenders."

23. Mitchell, "666 Jelly Doughnuts?"

24. Sutton, "Student Holds Up Captiol."

25. Hinson interview.

26. "Student Barricades Himself in Office."

27. See Davies, "An Appetite for Failure"; and "Student Fed Up to the Teeth."

28. Cohen interview.

29. Bruns, "Weak Link," 4A.

30. Vasilinda, "Raw Footage."

31. Graham interview.

32. Kling, "Psychological Report," 4.

33. Ibid.

34. Vasilinda interview.

35. Graham interview.

36. Mitchell, "666 Jelly Doughnuts?" 1.

37. Sutton, "Student Holds Up Capitol," 1B.

38. Van Gieson and Yeomans, "Intruder Disrupts Capitol," 1.

39. Mitchell, "666 Jelly Doughnuts?" 7.

40. Judd, "Eight Hour Siege Ends."

41. "Exhibit I," Oral Statement from Marshall Robin Ledbetter Jr., June 14, 1991, 3, State of Florida v. Marshall Ledbetter, Case No. 91-2027, Leon County Courthouse, Tallahassee, Florida. Hereafter cited as Florida v. Ledbetter.

42. Ibid.

43. Ibid., 4.

44. Steven Profit declined to be interviewed for this book.

45. Matus interview, April 24, 2013.

46. Josh Mitchell, e-mail to author, April 21, 2013.

47. Matus interview, April 24, 2013.

48. Josh Mitchell, e-mail to author, April 21, 2013.

49. Arvesen interview.

50. Andrew Afrvesen, e-mail to author, April 24, 2013.

51. Mahler interview.

52. Ibid.

53. Vasilinda, "Capitol Showdown."

Chapter 10. Searching for an Explanation

1. Peppe interview.

2. Biafra interview.

3. Katz, *Seductions of Crime*, 7, emphasis in original.

4. The term *perp walk* refers to the practice of law enforcement escorting alleged perpetrators of crimes from one location (e.g., the scene of a crime) to another (e.g., a detention facility). While some of these rituals take place away from the prying eyes of the media, others occur in public view and are fraught with symbolism.

5. Katz, *Seductions of Crime*, 2, 7.

6. Vasilinda, "Raw Footage."

7. Kilmister, *White Line Fever*, 2.

8. Kester, *Dead Kennedys*, 40.

9. See Lasn, *Culture Jam*.

10. Tedlock, "The Clown's Way," 105. I thank Brian Siegel for drawing my attention to Tedlock's work.

11. Ibid.

12. Ibid., 115.

13. Leary, *Flashbacks*, 31.

14. Cohen interview.

15. Mitchell, "666 Jelly Doughnuts?" 6.

16. Judd, "Eight Hour Siege Ends," 1A.

17. Hinson, "18 Years Ago," B1.

18. Thompson, "Freak Power in the Rockies," 32.

19. Merton, "Social Structure and Anomie."

20. Riley and Blackman, "Between Prohibitions," 63.

21. Ron Matus, e-mail to author, October 13, 2010.

22. Peppe interview.

23. Ibid.

24. "All about Wampum," http://web.grinnell.edu/courses/edu/f01/edu315 -01/liberato/wampum.html.

25. Chaudhuri and Chaudhuri, *Sacred Path*, 29.

26. Ibid., 34.

27. Zinn, *People's History*, 126.

28. Ibid.

29. This is according to a memorial located at the site.

30. Mitchell, "666 Jelly Doughnuts?" 7.

31. Ibid.

32. Hunter S. Thompson, who is not mentioned in Ledbetter's demands note, was also an inspiration. Oddly, Marshall does not demand a date with Paula Abdul.

33. Kilmister, *White Line Fever*, 70.

34. "What I've Learn't: Lemmy," October 27, 2012, http://www.thetimes.co .uk/tto/magazine/article3576022.ece.

35. Harmetz, "Singer's Trial," 17.

36. Smart, "Dead Kennedys Surface in Capital," C4.

37. Boose interview.

38. Smith and Warrior, *Like a Hurricane*, 138.

39. Ibid., 167.

40. Ibid., 157.

41. Ibid., 158.

42. Athens quoted in Rhodes, *Why They Kill*, 275–76.

43. Ibid., 84.

Chapter 11. Incompetent to Proceed

1. Spence, "Court-Ordered Psychological Evaluation," July 2, 1991, 5.

2. Healy, *Mania*, 88.

3. Jamison, *Touched with Fire*, 248.

4. Baldessarini et al., "Is Lithium Still Worth Using?" 69.

5. Ghaemi, *A First-Rate Madness*, 254.

6. Mitchell, "666 Jelly Doughnuts?" 2.

7. Jamison, *Touched with Fire*, 242.

8. Mitchell, "666 Jelly Doughnuts?" 2.

9. "Motion to Set Bail," June 19, 1991, 1–2, Florida v. Ledbetter.

10. Associated Press, "Tests Ordered for Senate Intruder."

11. Ibid.

12. Mitchell, "Psychological Tests," 5.

13. Ibid.

14. Ibid.

15. "Conditional Plea of Not Guilty," June 21, 1991, Florida v. Ledbetter.

16. Mitchell, "One Flew," 26.

17. Ibid.

18. Ibid.

19. Ibid.

20. Spence, "Court-Ordered Psychological Evaluation," July 2, 1991, 3.

21. Files, "Vehement Disgust," 4.

22. Ibid.

23. Harris, "Where's the Humor?" 4.

24. Murrell interview.

25. Ibid.

26. Ibid.

27. Spence, "Court-Ordered Psychological Evaluation," July 2, 1991, 2.

28. Ibid.

29. Ibid.

30. Ibid., 4.

31. Given his other antics, it is surprising that Ledbetter didn't file a motion to act as his own attorney.

32. Spence, "Court-Ordered Psychological Evaluation," July 2, 1991, 4.

33. Ibid., 3.

34. Ibid., 4.

35. Ibid.

36. Raskin, *Revolution for the Hell of It*, 205.

37. Spence, "Court-Ordered Psychological Evaluation," July 2, 1991, 5.

38. Ibid., 4.

39. Ibid., 6.

40. Kling, "Psychological Report," 4–5.

41. Ibid., 5.

42. Ibid., 6–7.

43. Ibid., 9.

44. Ibid., 5–6.

45. Ibid., 6.

46. Ibid., 4, 9.

47. Ibid., 9.

48. Ibid., 8.

49. Ibid.

50. Ibid.

51. Ibid.

52. Ibid., 9.

53. Randy Murrell to Marshall Ledbetter, July 22, 1991, Florida v. Ledbetter.

54. "Order Finding Defendant Incompetent to Proceed and Committing Defendant to Florida State Hospital," July 23, 1991, Florida v. Ledbetter.

55. Mitchell, "Ledbetter Sent to State Hospital," 1.

56. Associated Press, "Capitol Intruder Ruled Unfit," 4B.

57. Jamison, *Touched with Fire*, 3.

58. Ghaemi, *A First-Rate Madness*, 12–13, 15.

59. Jamison, *Touched with Fire*, 3.

60. Ibid.

61. Ghaemi, *A First-Rate Madness*, 3.

62. Leary, *Flashbacks*, 33.

63. Jamison, *Touched with Fire*, 105.

64. Morse interview.

65. Mitchell interview.

Chapter 12. Chattahoochee

1. Matthiessen, *Shadow Country*.

2. "Florida State Hospital," http://www.dcf.state.fl.us/facilities/fsh/docs/psy intern.pdf.

3. Carey, "With Toughness and Caring," F6.

4. "Florida State Hospital."

5. Ibid.

6. Ibid.

7. Morse interview.

8. Schwartz, "Competency Evaluation," 3.

9. Ibid.

10. Jonathan Lammers, e-mail to author, May 7, 2013. Although Lammers said Marshall had told him it was due to the medicine he was taking, Marshall wasn't taking any medication at the time. Ledbetter was crying.

11. Boehmke interview.

12. Schwartz, "Competency Evaluation," 3.

13. Mitchell interview.

14. Mitchell, "One Flew," 26.

15. Ibid., 25.

16. Ibid.

17. Ibid., 26.

18. Ibid.

19. Ibid.

20. Ibid.

21. Ibid.

22. Ibid.

23. Ibid.

24. Ibid.

25. Ibid.

26. Mitchell interview.

27. Sanz, Wilbur, and Boose, "Losing His Mind," 4.

28. Ibid.

29. Ibid.

30. Ibid.

31. Pudlow, "Resistance to Treatment," 1A.

32. Ibid.

33. Ibid., 10A.

34. Mitchell, "Ledbetter Must Take Lithium," 3.

35. Mitchell, "Ledbetter Refuses Lithium Treatment," 2.

36. Ibid.

37. Pudlow, "Resistance to Treatment," 10A.

38. Associated Press, "Capitol Intruder Ruled Unfit," 4B.

39. Mitchell, "Ledbetter Refuses Lithium Treatment," 2.

40. Ibid.

41. Ibid.

Chapter 13. Recovery

1. Lustig, "Discouraged Ledbetter Attempts to Break Out," 1.

2. Ibid., 5.

3. Ibid.

4. Ibid.

5. Ibid.

6. Ibid.

7. Lustig, "Ledbetter Begins Voluntarily Taking Prozac," 2.

8. Ibid.

9. Schwartz, "Competency Evaluation," 3–4.

10. Ibid., 4.

11. Ibid.

12. Ibid.

13. Ibid.

14. Ibid., 3.

15. Ibid., 7.

16. Ibid.

17. Biafra interview.

18. Torbett, "Biafra Comes Out Swinging," 5.

19. Mitchell, "Hyper-Activist Lands Safely Home," 5.

20. "Order Granting Pretrial Release," January 3, 1991, Florida v. Ledbetter.

21. Lammers quoted in Mitchell, "Hyper-Activist Lands Safely Home," 5.

Chapter 14. Busted

1. Mitchell, "Hyper-Activist Lands Safely Home," 5.

2. Ibid.

3. Ibid.

4. Ibid.

5. Ibid.

6. Ibid.

7. In a "Tales of Psychoboy" entry from October 4, 1996, Ledbetter said he was tired of having to "answer the inevitable question—'Why'd you do that back in '91?'"—which "occurs *every* time I meet someone I haven't seen since high school."

8. *Florida Statutes*, 810.023.

9. "Order Withholding Adjudication of Guilt and Placing Defendant on Probation," February 27, 1992, Florida v. Ledbetter.

10. Ibid.

11. In a "Tales of Psychoboy" entry from October 1, 1996, Ledbetter wrote: "FSU dropped me like Saul on the road to Damascus."

12. Peppe interview.

13. Mizelle, "Violation Report Form," 1.

14. Spence, "Court-Ordered Psychological Evaluation," May 31, 1994, 4.

15. Mizelle, "Violation Report Form," 2.

16. Carr, "Man Who Barricaded Himself."

17. Spence, "Court-Ordered Psychological Evaluation," May 31, 1994, 4.

18. Mizelle, "Violation Report Form," 2.

19. Spence, "Court-Ordered Psychological Evaluation," May 31, 1994, 3.

20. Ibid., 4.

21. "Motion to Determine Competency to Proceed," May 26, 1994, 1, Florida v. Ledbetter.

22. The center might have been an option for Ledbetter in 1991 had the initial charges filed against him been less severe.

23. Spence, "Court-Ordered Psychological Evaluation," May 31, 1994, 1.

24. Ibid., 2.

25. Ibid.

26. Ibid., 3.

27. Ibid., 4.

28. Ibid.

29. Sharon Graham, e-mail to author, April 12, 2014.

30. Spence, "Court-Ordered Psychological Evaluation," May 31, 1994, 4.

31. Ibid., 6.

32. Ibid.

33. McClaren, "Forensic Psychological Evaluation," 1.

34. Ibid., 2.

35. Ibid.

36. Ibid.

37. Ibid.

38. "Motion for Determination of Defendant's Competency to Proceed and Waiver of Hearing," June 22, 1994, Florida v. Ledbetter.

39. Tschinkel interview.

40. Hinson interview.

41. Ibid.

42. MacQueen interview.

43. "Amended Order Modifying Probation," February 8, 1995, Florida v. Ledbetter.

Chapter 15. "Tales of Psychoboy"

1. This is a pseudonym.

2. This is a pseudonym.

3. Jonathan Lammers, e-mail to author, May 7, 2013.

4. In 2004 Stoecklin was awarded a PhD in management information systems from Florida State University. She married, had a son, and was living in Tallahassee. She died unexpectedly in June 2006.

5. Krawchuk interview. In a "Tales of Psychoboy" entry from September 23, 1996, Ledbetter explained his plight: "I am trying to escape my karma cycle, and my dharma is definitely not at Marshall's Camera, AKA The Dusty, Fluorescent Lights Cellblock. Ugh."

6. Ledbetter, "Tales of Psychoboy," August 17, 1996.

7. The reference is to the Englishman who worked as a double agent for the Soviets in the 1950s. Blake escaped London's Wormwood Scrubs prison in 1966 and fled to the Soviet Union, where he lives. He was given a state pension that he enjoys to this day.

8. Ledbetter, "Tales of Psychoboy," August 20, 1996.

9. Ibid., August 21, 1996. Marshall would add, as an aside, "Plus the old guy had a problem with beer in the fridge."

10. Ibid.

11. Ibid., August 27, 1996.

12. Ibid.

13. Ibid., September 23, 1996.

14. Ibid., September 20, 1996.

15. Ibid., September 4, 1996.

16. Ibid., September 5, 1996.

17. Ibid., September 24, 1996.

18. Ibid., September 18, 1996.

19. Ibid., September 24, 1996.

20. Ibid.

21. Ibid., December 29, 1996.

22. Ibid.

23. Biafra interview.

24. Ibid.

25. "Jello Biafra," Music News of the World, accessed September 17, 2013, http://sniggle.net/Jello/jb3.php.

26. Biafra interview.

27. Krawchuk interview.

28. Alicia Calandra, e-mail to author, June 6, 2013.

29. Calandra interview.

30. Alicia Calandra, e-mail to author, April 22, 2013.

31. Alicia Calandra, e-mail to author, April 24, 2013.

32. Ledbetter, "Tales of Psychoboy," September 4, 1996.

33. Alicia Calandra, e-mail to author, August 9, 2013.

34. This is a pseudonym.

35. Arbaugh interview, April 26, 2013.

36. Arbaugh interview, April 15, 2011.

37. In a "Tales of Psychoboy" entry from October 1, 1996, Marshall signs off by saying: "I'll mail all this tomorrow if my disability check comes in to the fund the postage."

38. Marshall Ledbetter, letter to the editor, *High Times*, December 1996, 8.

Chapter 16. Al-Qaeda and the Blue Key Club

1. Marty Clear, "Communities Step Up Where State Left Off in Treatment of Mentally Ill," 2008, Tampa Bay Medical News, http://www.tampabaymedical news.com/content/communities-step-up-where-state-left-off-in-treatment-for-mentally-ill.

2. Walsh, "Psychiatric Hospital Loses Its Leader," 1B.

3. Gentry, "Report Critical of Mental Hospital," 1B.

4. Ibid.

5. Trontz, "Hospital Slams Door on Records." 1.

6. Florida Department of Law Enforcement Investigative Report, Case No. PO-73-0445, May 10, 2002.

7. Florida Department of Law Enforcement Investigative Report (Draft), Case No. PO-73-0446, no date.

8. Culture jamming is a media-savvy protest movement that aims to subvert everyday life as a form of resistance to the power and domination of consumerist society. See Lasn, *Culture Jam.*

9. Pimp Daddy Welfare (aka PDW), a tall, nerdy, white rapper with an interest in mathematics, bore an uncanny resemblance to Marshall. On his website, Ledbetter called him the "BEST rapper on the planet."

10. As of April 5, 2014, a list of all of Ledbetter's rants except those from 2002 was available at http://web.archive.org/web/20011221082041/http://marshallledbetter.com/archives.html. Three of the rants can be accessed in their entirety at http://web.archive.org/web/20011204030444/http://marshallledbetter.com.

11. Ledbetter made copies of the rants after he posted them. One set (along with the August–December 1996 issues of "Tales of Psychoboy") ended up in the hands of his friend Kyle Bermingham, who graciously shared them with the author in September 2013.

12. Ledbetter, "Full-On Drunk Rant."

13. Ibid.

14. In his "Tales of Psychoboy" entry for October 1, 1996, Ledbetter noted: "At FSU I saw countless students being programmed daily. They walked to class, eyes straight ahead, gait tightly controlled. That was what I loved about science. The code was not sacred. . . . I think that's the basic difference between a free-thinker and a dogmatist. One's banging out code, the other is receiving and repeating it."

15. Ledbetter, "Flossing."

16. Ibid.

17. Ibid.

18. Ledbetter, "Advice for Aspiring Messiahs."

19. Ibid.

20. Ibid.

21. Ibid. On the question of whether or not Ledbetter thought he was Jesus Christ, see "What Would Jesus Drink?" (August 4, 2001), where Ledbetter writes: "Anyway, that's enough about Jesus. He is out there. Except that he's in some mental facility currently, being forcibly medicated and subjected to a 're-education' regimen along with a motley assortment of other unfortunates for the crime of telling a post-secondary-institution-trained 'mental health professional' his actual name. (Possibly his crime was/is believing that was/is his name. The mental health field enforces the copyright Jesus has on his name. You can use his name, but don't be his name). . . . Just for the record, if any post-secondary-institution-trained 'mental health professionals' do happen to read this, please allow me let to firmly stress the following—not only is my given name Marshall Robin Ledbetter, Jr., I honestly and totally believe that I am Marshall Robin Ledbetter, Jr. . . . Even more importantly, I absolutely believe I am not Jesus. After all, his name has two syllables and mine has nine, and they're different syllables, too."

22. Ledbetter, "Arcadia."

23. Ibid.

24. Ibid.

25. Ibid.

26. Ibid.

27. Ibid.

28. Krueger, "State Mental Hospital Shuts Down."

29. Ibid., 4B.

30. This was not be the final end of the facility. It was soon transformed into the Desoto County Juvenile Correctional Complex, with three hundred male and female juvenile offenders and four hundred employees. Nine years later, in 2011, that facility was shut down by the Florida Legislature. At the time of writing the property is vacant.

31. Ledbetter, "Tales of Psychoboy," September 26, 1996.

32. Ledbetter, "The Al Aqsa Martyrs' Brigade."

33. Florida Department of Law Enforcement Investigative Report, Case No. PO-73-0445, May 10, 2002.

34. Ibid.

35. Ibid.

36. "Directory of Services," 2009–2010, 3, http://www.peace-river.com/User Files/Directory%20of%20Services%2010.pdf.

37. Tallahassee Regional Security Task Force, BOLO Flyer Regarding Marshall Ledbetter, May 10, 2002.

38. Florida Department of Law Enforcement Investigative Report, Case No. PO-73-0445, May 15, 2002.

39. Ibid.

Chapter 17. Exit

1. In grieving with other members of the family soon after Marshall's death, Sharon Graham says they all came to realize that in his last days Marshall had made a successful effort to spend quality time alone with each member of his immediate family. "In retrospect, I believe he was saying good-bye," she says. Sharon Graham, e-mail to author, April 13, 2014.

2. Fisher, "What Makes America's Gun Culture Totally Unique."

3. S. Anderson, "The Urge to End It All."

4. Jamison, Touched with Fire, 58.

5. Sharon Graham, e-mail to author, April 13, 2014.

6. S. Anderson, "The Urge to End It All."

7. Ledbetter, "America's Runaway Train," 4A.

8. S. Anderson, "The Urge to End It All."

9. Ibid.

10. Bermingham interview.

11. Ibid.

12. Ibid.

13. Ibid.

14. Marshall Ledbetter to Livia Ledbetter, June 11, 2002.

15. Marshall's mother says that there are only two people who might know what sort of treatment Marshall underwent at Peace River: Marshall Ledbetter Sr. and a mental-health "advocate who helped [Marshall Jr.] adjust to living on his own." She says that right after being deinstitutionalized from Chattahoochee, "Marshall was released into the care of his father [who] was named as the one who was allowed to have medical information." However, "at the end of his life he was not in the custody of his father, he was under direction [of] an advocate named to his case." Marshall's mother says that she does not know whether, during Marshall's last visit to the Peace River Center, "Marshall, Sr. was still being informed of our son's medical treatment or the drugs prescribed him." Mr. Ledbetter has declined to comment. The identity of Marshall's state-appointed mental-health advocate is unknown. Sharon Graham, e-mail to author, April 26, 2014.

16. Sharon Graham, e-mail to author, April 13, 2014.

17. Bermingham interview.

18. Williams, *Blue Rage, Black Redemption*, 224.

19. Bermingham interview.

20. Arbaugh interview, April 26, 2013.

21. Ibid.

22. Ibid.

23. Bermingham interview.

Chapter 18. Making Sense of Marshall Ledbetter

1. Hester interview.

2. Judt, *Ill Fares the Land*, 178.

3. Durkheim, *The Division of Labor in Society*.

4. Arvesen interview.

5. This view has not been without its critics. David Healy reminds us that it was not long ago that schizophrenia, rather than bipolar disorder, was thought to contain the kernel of truth in explaining the artistic mind: "There are good reasons to remain skeptical of all proposed links, whether to manic-depressive illness or to schizophrenia" (*Mania*, 151).

6. Angell, "The Epidemic of Mental Illness," 22.

7. Ibid.

8. In the *North Carolina Defender Manual,* Rubin and Grine caution lawyers against being too hasty in pursuing a decision of incompetence to proceed and suggest that doing so "may stigmatize a Defendant" (chapter 2, page 13).

9. Kroska and Harkness, "Coping with the Stigma," 1315.

10. Audie Cornish, "Psychiatrists to Take New Approach in Bereavement," December 6, 2012, http://www.npr.org/2012/12/06/166682774/psychiatrists-to-take-new-approach-in-bereavement.

11. See Parenti, *The Culture Struggle,* chapter 4

12. Ledbetter, "Tales of Psychoboy," October 4, 1996.

13. Jamison, *Touched with Fire,* 58.

14. S. Anderson, "The Urge to End It All."

15. Ledbetter, "11/17/01."

16. Ashton et al. "Cannabinoids in Bipolar Affective Disorder," 298.

17. Grob et al., "Pilot Study of Psilocybin Treatment," 71.

18. Ibid.

19. Marshall would be fascinated by religious thought and expression throughout his life. His own beliefs may be captured most succinctly in a "Tales of Psychoboy" entry dated October 19, 1996: "I truly believe that the greatest problem in the Western world today is the unbelievable influence of the Judeo-Christian ethos where, so often, life is defined by those holding power in church/state positions as black/white. Good/evil. Unambiguous. Even when I had my explosion it was couched in an Old Testament style context. I'll be sticking to Buddhism from now on."

20. Ledbetter, "Tales of Psychoboy," September 30, 1996.

21. Hinson, "18 Years Ago," B1.

22. Campbell interview.

23. It is interesting that Strickland's comments to the press and her rather upbeat interpretation of Ledbetter's motives and behavior never again entered official conversation (what James Scott calls the "public transcripts") about why Marshall occupied the capitol that day.

24. Matus interview, October 3, 2010.

25. Ron Matus, e-mail to author, May 12, 2013.

26. Ibid.

27. Matus continues, "I think I need that lesson now more than ever." Yet he confesses that he is now much more skeptical of political change. "Getting older, and being a reporter, has made me better see how complicated the world can be." Matus says that since the early 1990s his political positions "have evolved because I'm hardwired to follow not only my heart and values, but the evidence as best I can determine it." Unlike during his younger days, he is now "more reluctant to join any bandwagon. . . . I see too many of them, of all stripes, chugging

along because of myths and misinformation, tribal politics, shallow thinking, special interest manipulation, etc." Ibid.

28. In 1998 the *Florida Flambeau* was bought out by its competitor, the *FS-View*. While the former name is still listed on the paper's masthead, the critical perspectives and tenacious reporting for which the *Flambeau* was so well known have vanished (for the most part) in the merger.

29. Josh Mitchell, e-mail to author, April 21, 2013.

30. Arvesen interview.

31. Jonathan Lammers, e-mail to author, May 7, 2013.

32. Ledbetter, "Tales of Psychoboy," October 1, 1996.

33. Ibid., October 3, 1996.

34. Ibid., October 11, 1996.

35. Ibid., November 11, 1996.

36. The magazine was apparently called *Eleven* and was associated with the University of Central Florida. It no longer seems to be in existence. It is not known if Ledbetter's story was ever published.

37. See Marshall Ledbetter, letter to the editor, *High Times*, December 1996, 8; and Ledbetter, "America's Runaway Train," 4A.

38. Ledbetter, "Tales of Psychoboy," October 6, 1996.

39. Murray, *Aldous Huxley*, 430.

40. Matus interview, October 3, 2010.

41. MacQueen interview.

42. Hinson, "18 Years Ago."

Bibliography

Interviews

Arbaugh, Conrad [pseud.]. Personal interview with author, April 15, 2011, Winter Haven, Florida.

————. Phone interview with author, April 26, 2013.

Arvesen, Andrew. Phone interview with author, March 15, 2012.

Bermingham, Kyle. Phone interview with author, September 7, 2013.

Biafra, Jello. Phone interview with author, June 26, 2013.

Boehmke, Jasper [pseud.]. Phone interview with author, October 27, 2010.

Boose, Chris. Phone interview with author, November 6, 2010.

Calandra, Alicia. Personal interview with author, April 15, 2011, Auburndale, Florida.

Campbell, Larry. Phone interview with author, November 5, 2010.

Cohen, Gregory. Phone interview with author, May 30, 2011.

Dennis, Ruby. Personal interview with author, May 20, 2011, Tallahassee, Florida.

Fuqua, Julie. Phone interview with author, November 18, 2010.

Graham, Sharon [formerly Sharon Ledbetter]. Phone interview with author, March 20, 2014.

Griffin, John. Phone interview with author, March 31, 2009.

Hester, Gary. Phone interview with author, June 20, 2011.

Hinson, Mark. Phone interview with author, October 17, 2010.

Krawchuk, Fritz [pseud.]. Phone interview with author, November 17, 2010.

Lovett, Jesse. Phone interview with author, May 20, 2011.

MacQueen, Steve. Phone interview with author, November 11, 2010.

Mahler, Lanora [pseud.]. Phone interview with author, October 19, 2010.

Matus, Ron. Phone interviews with author, October 3, 2010, and April 24, 2013.

Mitchell, Josh. Phone interview with author, June 30, 2011.

Morse, Tracy. Personal interview with author, May 21, 2011, Tallahassee, Florida.

Murrell, Randolph. Phone interview with author, October 25, 2010.

Peppe, Bert [pseud.]. Phone interview with author, September 29, 2010.

Pepperman, Bradley [pseud.]. Phone interview with author, November 12, 2010.

Todd, Wayne. Phone interview with author, September 28, 2010.

Tschinkel, Walter. Phone interview with author, October 23, 2010.

Vasilinda, Mike. Phone interview with author, October 18, 2010.

Witherspoon, Eric. Phone interview with author, June 2, 2013.

Sources

Anderson, Curt. "They Rapped about Bugs and Budgets." *St. Petersburg Times*, June 20, 1991.

Anderson, Scott. "The Urge to End It All." *New York Times*, July 6, 2008, http://www.nytimes.com/2008/07/06/magazine/06suicide-t.html?pagewanted=all&_r=0.

Angell, Marcia. "The Epidemic of Mental Illness: Why?" *New York Review of Books*, June 23, 2011.

Ashton, C. H., P. B. Moore, P. Gallagher, and A. H. Young. "Cannabinoids in Bipolar Affective Disorder: A Review and Discussion of Their Therapeutic Potential." *Journal of Psychopharmacology* 19, no. 3 (2005): 293–300.

Associated Press. "Architect, State Officials, Clash on Capitol Design." *Daytona Beach Morning Journal*, March 16, 1971.

———. "Capitol Intruder Refuses to Take Lithium at Hospital." *St. Petersburg Times,* September 10, 1991.

———. "Capitol Intruder Ruled Unfit." *St. Petersburg Times*, July 25, 1991.

———. "Tests Ordered for Senate Intruder." *St. Petersburg Times*, June 21, 1991.

———. "Wants Vote on Capitol Reversed." *Daytona Beach Morning Journal*, May 18, 1971.

Baldessarini, Ross J., L. Tondo, J. Hennen, and A. C. Viquera. "Is Lithium Still Worth Using?" *Harvard Review of Psychiatry* 10, no. 2 (2002): 59–75.

Bennett, Hal Zina. *Zuni Fetishes*. San Francisco: Harper, 1993.

Book of the SubGenius: Lunatic Prophecies for the Coming Weird Times. New York: McGraw-Hill, 1983.

Bruns, Dave. "Weak Link in Security Was Exploited." *Tallahassee Democrat*, June 15, 1991.

Campbell, Joseph. *The Power of Myth*. New York: Anchor, 1991.

Carey, Benedict. "With Toughness and Caring, a New Therapy Helps Tortured Souls." *New York Times*, July 13, 2004.

Carr, Susan Latham. "Man Who Barricaded Himself in Capitol in '91 Is Arrested Again." *Tallahassee Democrat*, May 17, 1994.

Chaudhuri, Jean, and Joyotpaul Chaudhuri. *A Sacred Path: The Way of the Muscogee Creeks*. Los Angeles: UCLA American Indian Studies Center, 2009.

Cotterell, Bill. "Senate Sergeant-at-Arms Retires after 30 Years." Associated Press, June 26, 1999.

Davies, R. "An Appetite for Failure." *Queensland Sunday Mail*, June 16, 1991.

Dick, Philip K. *The Divine Invasion*. Boston: Mariner Books, 2011.

———. *A Scanner Darkly*. Boston: Mariner Books, 2011.

———. *The Transmigration of Timothy Archer*. Boston: Mariner Books, 2011.

Durkheim, Émile. *The Division of Labor in Society*. New York: Free Press, 1984.

Feynman, Richard P. *"Surely You're Joking Mr. Feynman!" Adventures of a Curious Character*. New York: Norton, 1985.

Files, Craig S. "Vehement Disgust." *Florida Flambeau*, July 1, 1991.

Fisher, Max. "What Makes America's Gun Culture Totally Unique, in Four Charts." *Washington Post*, December 15, 2012.

Gentry, Carol. "Report Critical of Mental Hospital." *St. Petersburg Times*, March 26, 1989.

Ghaemi, Nassir. *A First-Rate Madness: Uncovering the Links between Leadership and Mental Illness*. New York: Penguin, 2011.

Gorightly, Adam. *The Prankster and the Conspiracy*. New York: Paraview Press, 2003.

Griffiths, Ronald R., M. Johnson, W. Richards, B. Richards, U. McCann, and R. Jesse. "Psilocybin Occasioned Mystical Experiences: Immediate and Persisting Dose-Related Effects." *Psychopharmacology* 218 (2011): 649–65.

Grob, Charles S., Alicia L. Danforth, Gurpreet S. Chopra, Marycie Hagarty, Charles R. McKay, Adam L. Halberstadt, and George R. Greer. "Pilot Study of Psilocybin Treatment for Anxiety in Patients with Advanced-Stage Cancer." *Archives of General Psychiatry* 68 (2011): 71–78.

Hallenbeck, Brent. "New Artistic Director Steve MacQueen Brings Work Ethic to Flynn Center." *Burlington Free Press*, December 6, 2012.

Hallifax, Jackie. "Man Barricades Himself in Florida Senate Office; Surrenders after Standoff." Associated Press, June 14, 1991.

———. "Man Surrenders after Barricading Self in Fla. Senate Office Building." Associated Press, June 14, 1991.

Harmetz, Aljean. "Singer's Trial on Nudity in Album Begins Today." *New York Times*, August 10, 1987.

Harris, Ingemar. "Where's the Humor?" *Florida Flambeau*, July 8, 1991.

Healy, David. *Mania: A Short History of Bipolar Disorder.* Baltimore: Johns Hopkins University Press, 2008.

Heidegger, Martin. "Why Do I Stay in the Provinces?" In *Martin Heidegger: The Man and the Thinker*, ed. Thomas Sheehan, 27–29. Piscataway: Transaction, 2009.

Hensley, Scott. "Study Finds No Link between Hallucinogens and Mental Problems." National Public Radio, August 20, 2013, http://www.npr.org /blogs/health/2013/08/19/213550995/study-finds-no-link-between-hallu cinogens-and-mental-problems.

Hinson, Mark. "18 Years Ago, Legendary Ledbetter Owned the Capitol." *Tallahassee Democrat*, June 14, 2009.

Horowitz, Helen Lefkowitz. *Campus Life: Undergraduate Cultures from the End of the Eighteenth Century to the Present.* Chicago: University of Chicago Press, 1987.

Hunting, Mary Anne. *Edward Durell Stone.* New York: Norton, 2013.

James, William. *The Varieties of Religious Experience: A Study in Human Nature.* New York: Signet, 1958.

Jamison, Kay Redfield. *Touched with Fire: Manic-Depressive Illness and the Artistic Temperament.* New York: Simon and Shuster, 1993.

Judd, Alan. "Eight Hour Siege Ends with Cigar, but No Pizza." *Sarasota Herald-Tribune*, June 15, 1991.

Judt, Tony. *Ill Fares the Land.* New York: Penguin, 2010.

Kastner, Susan. "Leary's in Town." *Toronto Star*, June 30, 1991.

Katz, Jack. *Seductions of Crime.* New York: Basic Books, 1988.

Kester, Marian. *Dead Kennedys: The Unathorized Version.* San Francisco: Last Gasp, 2003.

Kilmister, Lemmy. *White Line Fever: The Autobiography.* New York: Kensington, 2002.

Kling, J. Kenneth. "Psychological Report." State of Florida v. Marshall Ledbetter. Case No. 91-2027, Leon County Courthouse, Tallahassee, Florida. July 15, 1991.

Kroska, Amy, and Sarah K. Harkness. "Coping with the Stigma of Mental Illness." *Social Forces* 89, no. 4 (2011): 1315–40.

Krueger, Curtis. "State Mental Hospital Shuts Down." *St. Petersburg Times*, February 9, 2002.

Lasn, Kalle. *Culture Jam: The Uncooling of America.* New York: William Morrow, 1999.

Leary, Timothy. *Flashbacks.* Los Angeles: J. P. Tarcher, 1983.

Ledbetter, Marshall, Jr. "Advice for Aspiring Messiahs." Unpublished weblog, October 17, 2001.

———. "The Al Aqsa Martyrs' Brigade." Unpublished weblog, March 21, 2002.

———. "America's Runaway Train Offers No Avenue of Escape." *Winter Haven News Chief*, October 26, 1996, 4A.

———. "Arcadia." Unpublished weblog, February 5, 2002.

———. "Flossing." Unpublished weblog, October 8, 2001.

———. "Full-On Drunk Rant." October 21, 2001. http://web.archive.org/web/20011204030444/http://marshallledbetter.com.

———. "Tales of Psychoboy." Unpublished manuscript, 1996.

———. "11-17-01." November 17, 2001. http://web.archive.org/web/20011204030444/http://marshallledbetter.com.

Lewis, John. *Walking with the Wind: A Memoir of the Movement*. New York: Harcourt Brace, 1998.

Lustig, Lauren V. "Discouraged Ledbetter Attempts to Break Out." *Florida Flambeau*, September 26, 1991.

———. "Ledbetter Begins Voluntarily Taking Prozac." *Florida Flambeau*, November 6, 1991.

MacLean, Katherine, Matthew W. Johnson, and Roland R. Griffiths. "Mystical Experiences Occasioned by the Hallucinogen Psilocybin Lead to Increases in the Personality Domain of Openness." *Journal of Psychopharmacology* 25 (2011): 1453–1561.

Marks, Kathy. "The Sixties Hero Who 'Turned On' a Generation." *The Independent (London)*, March 15, 2011.

Matthiessen, Peter. *Shadow Country*. New York: Modern Library, 2008.

McClaren, Harry A. "Forensic Psychological Evaluation." State of Florida v. Marshall Ledbetter. Case No. 91-2027, Leon County Courthouse, Tallahassee, Florida. June 4, 1994.

McKenna, Terence. *Food of the Gods*. New York: Bantam, 1992.

Merton, Robert K. "Social Structure and Anomie." *American Sociological Review* 3, no. 5 (1938): 672–82.

Miller, Sam. *Capitol: A Guide for Visitors*. Tallahassee: Historic Tallahassee Preservation Board, 2008.

Mitchell, Josh. "Hyper-Activist Lands Safely Home." *Florida Flambeau*, January 8, 1992.

———. "Ledbetter Must Take Lithium to Stand Trial." *Florida Flambeau*, September 4, 1991.

———. "Ledbetter Refuses Lithium Treatment." *Florida Flambeau*, September 6, 1991.

———. "Ledbetter Sent to State Hospital after Being Declared Unfit for Trial." *Florida Flambeau*, July 25, 1991.

———. "One Flew Over the Cuckoo's Nest Part II." *Florida Flambeau*, August 19, 1991.

———. "Psychological Tests on Ledbetter Done; Hearing Date Set." *Florida Flambeau*, July 22, 1991.

———. "666 Jelly Doughnuts? Friends Insist Ledbetter Is No Loon." *Florida Flambeau*, June 17, 1991.

Mizelle, Marlon. "Violation Report Form." State of Florida v. Marshall Ledbetter. Case No. 91-2027, Leon County Courthouse, Tallahassee, Florida. May 13, 1994.

Murray, Nicholas. *Aldous Huxley*. New York: St. Martin's Press, 2002.

Myrie, Russell. *Don't Rhyme for the Sake of Riddlin': The Authorized Story of Public Enemy*. New York: Canongate, 2008.

Newberger, Devra. *The Magic of Paula Abdul*. New York: Scholastic, 1991.

Newell, Martin. *Wild Man of Wivenhoe*. Wivenhoe, Essex, UK: Jardine Press, 1996.

Parenti, Michael. *The Culture Struggle*. New York: Seven Stories Press, 2006.

Pizek, Jeff. "Becky Hemingway Makes Impressive Debut with 'Too Much Plenty.'" *Chicago Daily Herald*, March 23, 2000.

Pretti, John. "Roast the Leon County Sheriff." January 5, 2011, http://www.examiner.com/article/roast-the-leon-county-sheriff.

Pudlow, Jan. "Resistance to Treatment Confounds Doctors, Courts." *Tallahassee Democrat*, September 9, 1991.

Raskin, Jonah. *Revolution for the Hell of It*. Berkeley: University of California Press, 1996.

Ravenhurst, Omar Khayyam. *Principia Discordia*. Lexington: Pacific Publishing Studio, 2011.

Rhodes, Richard. *Why They Kill: The Discoveries of a Maverick Criminologist*. New York: Vintage Books, 1999.

Riley, Sarah C. E., and Graham Blackman. "Between Prohibitions: Patterns and Meanings of Magic Mushroom Use in the UK." *Substance Use and Misuse* 43 (2008): 55–71.

Roberts, Diane. "Tallahassee: Not the Florida You Know." *Washington Post*, April 8, 2007.

Rubin, John, and Alyson A. Grine. *North Carolina Defender Manual, Volume 1, Pretrial*. 2nd ed. Chapel Hill: School of Government, 2013.

Sanz, Erica, Paul Wilbur, and Chris Boose. "Losing His Mind." *Florida Flambeau*, August 29, 1991.

Savio, Mario. "Sproul Hall Steps, December 2, 1964." http://www.lib.berkeley
.edu/MRC/saviotranscript.html.

Schwartz, Jill. "Competency Evaluation." State of Florida v. Marshall Ledbetter. Case No. 91-2027, Leon County Courthouse, Tallahassee, Florida. November 4, 1991.

Scott, Danny. "I'm Not Saying I'm the Best Looking Bloke at the Bar." *Sunday Times Magazine,* May 19, 2013.

Scott, James C. *Domination and the Arts of Resistance.* New Haven: Yale University Press, 1992.

Sexton, Christine. "Guide to the Capitol: This Is Where the Action Is." *Florida Flambeau,* July 11, 1991.

———. "Looking for an Organic High? Jump a Fence and Try Fungi." *Florida Flambeau,* July 11, 1991.

Smart, Amy. "Dead Kennedys Surface in Capital." *Times Colonist,* September 29, 2012.

Smith, Paul Chaat, and Robert Allen Warrior. *Like a Hurricane: The Indian Movement from Alcatraz to Wounded Knee.* New York: New Press, 1996.

Spence, William. "Court-Ordered Psychological Evaluation." State of Florida v. Marshall Ledbetter. Case No. 91-2027, Leon County Courthouse, Tallahassee, Florida. July 2, 1991.

———. "Court-Ordered Psychological Evaluation." State of Florida v. Marshall Ledbetter. Case No. 91-2027, Leon County Courthouse, Tallahassee, Florida. May 31, 1994.

"Student Barricades Himself in Office." *Eugene Register-Guard*, June 15, 1991.

"Student Fed Up to the Teeth." *Sydney Sun Herald*, June 16 1991.

Sutton, Charlotte. "Student Holds Up Capitol." *St. Petersburg Times.* June 15, 1991.

Tedlock, Barbara. "The Clown's Way." In *Teachings from the American Earth: Indian Religion and Philosophy,* ed. Dennis Tedlock and Barbara Tedlock, 105–18. New York: Liveright, 1975.

Thompson, Hunter S. "Freak Power in the Rockies." *Rolling Stone,* October 1, 1970.

Torbett, Glen. "Biafra Comes Out Swinging." *Florida Flambeau*, November 13, 1991.

Trontz, Ian. "Hospital Slams Door on Records." *Tampa Tribune*, June 25, 1995.

Tymoczko, Dmitri. "The Nitrous Oxide Philosopher." *Atlantic Monthly*, May 1996.

United Press International. "Man Who Barricaded Himself in Capitol Needed 'Soapbox.'" June 15, 1991.

Van Gieson, John C., and Adam Yeomans. "Intruder Disrupts Capitol, Funniest Home Videos Fodder in Odd Standoff." *Orlando Sentinel,* June 15, 1991.

Vasilinda, Michael D. "Capitol Showdown—Part 3." Courtesy Mike Vasilinda Productions.

———. "Raw Footage: Marshall Ledbetter Saga at Florida State Capitol." Courtesy Mike Vasilinda Productions.

Walsh, Patricia. "Psychiatric Hospital Loses Its Leader." *Sarasota Herald-Tribune,* January 10, 2000.

Vonnegut, Kurt. *Jailbird.* New York: Doubleday, 1979.

———. *Slaughterhouse Five.* New York: Dell, 1991.

Wasson, R. Gordon. "Seeking the Magic Mushroom." *Life,* June 10, 1957.

Waters, Tamryn. "Campbell in Renewed Fight with Lung Cancer." *Tallahassee Democrat,* November 27, 2013.

Wells, John. "The Monarchical Dialectic." Unpublished manuscript, 1990.

Williams, Stanley Tookie. *Blue Rage, Black Redemption.* New York: Simon and Schuster, 2007.

Zinn, Howard. *A People's History of the United States.* New York: HarperPerennial, 1995.

Index

Page numbers in *italics* refer to illustrations.

"King Love" (Kamal Youssef), 8
Kirk, Grayson, 78
Kittrell, Chris, 82
Kling, J. Kenneth, 94–98, 103, 154
Kroska, Amy, 155
KRS-One, 50

Lakeland Ledger, 134, 150
Lammers, Jonathan, 9, 33, 115; friendship with Ledbetter, 161; on Ledbetter's fascination with Paula Abdul, 17; Monarchy Party, 20; "Mushroom Cop," 19; visiting Ledbetter in Chattahoochee, 104
Lanan, Hugh, 88
Landis Hall, 7, 16, 21, 68; Ledbetter coke machine incident at, 9–10; living arrangements at, 7
Lard (band), 125, 129–30
Leary, Timothy, 19, 130, 133; alleged death of, 62–63; influence on Ledbetter, 19, 62, 83–84; mentioned in Ledbetter's demands note, 52; psilocybin mushrooms, and, 25, 77, 100, 119
Ledbetter, Arlen, 4, 34, 118, 127, 150, 169n1
Ledbetter, Carla, 4, 34, 169n1
Ledbetter, Christina, 4, 9, 169n1
Ledbetter, Livia, 131, 147–48
Ledbetter, Marshall, Sr., 4–5, 34, 64, 121, 169n1
Ledbetter, Sharon, 4–6, 32, 125, 144, 154, 169n1
Ledbetter family, 9, 14, 32, 34, 65; interactions with the media, 66; trying to get help for Marshall, 32
Lennon, John, 19
Leon County, Fla., 8, 27, 33, 35, 51, 68
Leon County Court, 100, 115, 117, 123
Leon County Jail, 89–90, 101, 120
Leon County Sheriff's Office, 27, 51, 62; hostage negotiation team, 54; Ledbetter oral statement at, 67; managing the mentally ill, 159;

negotiations with Ledbetter, 58; transporting Ledbetter to Chattahoochee, 100
Lewis, John, 1
Life magazine, 25
Lifers, The, 15
Linklater, Richard, 14
Lithium, 88–9; Ledbetter's refusal to take, 89, 96, 106, 109–10, 112–13; side effects of, 88; as treatment for bipolar disorder, 88
Little, Nell, 5
Livings, John, 67
Los Angeles Times, 84
Lovett, Jesse, 2–3, 51, 57
LSD, 29–30, 119, 121, 149. *See also* Drugs
Lucky Strikes, 82–83
Lustig, Lauren, 111–12
Luther, Jennifer, 67

MacQueen, Steve, 21, 123, 163–64
Mandela, Nelson, 109
Manic depression. *See* Bipolar disorder
Manifest and latent functions, 73
Mann, Frank, 61
Mardi Gras, 23
Margolis, Gwen, 61
Marijuana, 11, 121, 129, 132; in Ledbetter's demands note, 52, 55, 83; libertarian politics, 156; treatment for bipolar disorder (manic depression), 158
Marshall's Camera, 4–5, 118–19, 125, 183n5
marshallledbetter.com, 135, 185n11
Marx, Karl, 10
Matus, Ron, 19, 68–69, 80, 160–61, 163
McClaren, Harry A., 122
McKenna, Terence, 23, 26, 28, 172n9
McPherson, James, 55, 61
McPherson, Tom, 61
MC Skat Kat, 17, 105, 171n14
Meadows, Mark, 27
Media, 3, 62–65, 70
Medical model, 72, 156

Mental health industry, 32, 71, 97–98, 138–40, 151, 156
Mental illness, 92; Ledbetter's diagnosis of, 94, 114, 145, 147, 151–51, 153; stigmatizing consequences of diagnosis, 155
Merry Pranksters, 14
Merton, Robert K., 73, 78–80
Metallica, 10
Mexico, 25
Miglino, Jo, 38–39
Mik, Dik, 84
Miles, William, 142
Ministry, 129
Mitchell, Josh, 66, 77, 88, 105, 116, 161
Mizelle, Marlon, 118–19
Mohammed, 138
Monarchy Party (FSU student government group), 20–22; on FSU campus, 21; and FSU strategic plan, 22; Ledbetter and, 22, 52, 63, 83, 128; response to capitol break-in, 68–70
Morgan, Lindee, 37–38
Morrison, Jim, 8, 170n14
Motörhead, 11, 29, 31–32, 75, 84
Mountain Goats, the, 13
MTV, 128
Murphy, Joy, 134
Murrell, Randolph, 99, 110; Ledbetter's attorney, 89–91, 96, 98, 120, 123; Ledbetter's release from Chattahoochee, 115
Muscogee Creeks, 24–25. See also Native Americans
"Mushroom Cop" (comic strip), 17, 18, 19, 69

NASA, 16
NASCAR racing, 132, 135–36
Native Americans, 17, 81, 85–86, 117, 170n13; ancestry in Ledbetter, 76, 121, 153; Red Sticks, 81; vision quest, 24–25, 76. See also Clown dancer
Newell, Martin, 172n18

New Orleans, 23–24
New York City, 75
N.W.A, 84
Nitrous oxide, 11, 23–24. See also Drugs

Ocala, Fla., 119
Occupy Wall Street, 75, 78
Office Pub (Winter Haven, Fla.), 146, 149–50
Ono, Yoko, 19
Organic solidarity, 153
Orlando, Fla., 118
Orlando Sentinel, 35, 43, 78
Ott-Laughlin Funeral Home, 150
"Ozymandias" (Shelley), 136

Payne, Rusty, 5
PCP, 149
Peace River Center (Bartow, Fla.), 141–43, 146–50, 154
Pensacola, Fla., 81
Phantom companions, 87
Pharmaceutical industry, 156
Pimp Daddy Welfare, 134
Polk Community College (Polk State College), 4, 6, 12
Polk County, Fla., 116, 118–19, 125–26, 128, 171n37
Pornography, 80, 157
Poverty, 64
Powell, Chuck, 20
Principia Discordia, 20, 125
Professional wrestling, 132
Profit, Steven, 42, 54, 68
Progressive Independent Party (PIP), 161
Prozac, 112
Psilocybin mushrooms, 11, 25–27, 121; counterculture, 25; effects of, 26, 28, 77, 79, 122; as inspiration for capitol break-in, 159; Ledbetter and, 23, 28–30, 37, 156–57; links to mental illness, 28; as metaphysical experience, 100, 158; treatment for depression,

Tuckabatchee, 81
Turner, Ted, 8

University of Florida, 6, 134
University of South Florida, 6
U.S. Capitol Police, 142
U.S. Secret Service, 105

Van Zandt, Townes, 116
Vasilinda, Mike, 55, 65; CNN broadcast
   of Ledbetter's demands, 57–58, 62,
   77; reporting of Ledbetter's arraign-
   ment, 71–72
Vause, Hansel, 67
Virtual reality, 14, 19, 39, 63, 84, 96
Vision quest, 23–30, 100, 136–38
Vonnegut, Kurt, 9, 170n20

Wacissa River, 56
Wakefield, Jerome, 155
Wampum, 80–81

Warrior, Robert, 86
Wasson, R. Gordon, 25
Wells, John, 21
WFLA television, 55
WFSU radio, 4, 38, 56
Whippets, 11, 23–24. *See also* Drugs
Wiggum, Clancy, 83
Wilbur, Paul, 105
Wild Man of Wivenhoe, 172n18
Williams, Stanley, 149
Winter Haven, Fla., 13, 127–28, 135; bar
   scene in, 128, 131, 146; hospital, 141;
   Ledbetter's place of birth, 4; Ledbet-
   ter as resident of, 143, 154
Winter Haven News Chief, 146
Witherspoon, Eric, 33, 37
Woodstock, 26
Woody Creek, Colo., 157
WVFS radio, 37

Yippies, 93

DANIEL M. HARRISON is associate professor of sociology at Lander University. His work has appeared in *Media, Culture and Society*, *Sexualities*, and *Contemporary Perspectives in Social Theory*. He lives in Greenwood, South Carolina, with his wife, artist Rebecca Harrison, and their two daughters, Liliana and Mirabel.